Be
Uncommon

Books by John Mason

An Enemy Called Average

Beat Self-Defeat

Believe You Can—The Power of a Positive Attitude

Be Yourself—Discover the Life You Were Meant to Live

Let Go of Whatever Holds You Back

Never Give Up—You're Stronger Than You Think

Proverbs Prayers

Seize Today

You Can Be Your Best—Starting Today

You Can Do It—Even If Others Say You Can't

You're Born an Original—Don't Die a Copy!

The Power of You

Be Uncommon

40 WAYS TO LEAVE AVERAGE BEHIND

John Mason

Revell

a division of Baker Publishing Group
Grand Rapids, Michigan

© 2023 by John Mason

Published by Revell
a division of Baker Publishing Group
PO Box 6287, Grand Rapids, MI 49516-6287
www.revellbooks.com

Printed in the United States of America

Library of Congress Cataloging-in-Publication Data
Names: Mason, John, 1955– author.
Title: Be uncommon : 40 ways to leave average behind / John Mason.
Description: Grand Rapids, MI : Revell, a division of Baker Publishing Group, 2023. | Includes bibliographical references.
Identifiers: LCCN 2022032655 | ISBN 9780800742904 (casebound) | ISBN 9780800738921 (paperback) | ISBN 9781493439799 (ebook)
Subjects: LCSH: Self-actualization—Religious aspects—Christianity. | Mediocrity.
Classification: LCC BV4598.2 .M265 2023 | DDC 158.1—dc23/eng/20220907
LC record available at https://lccn.loc.gov/2022032655

Baker Publishing Group publications use paper produced from sustainable forestry practices and post-consumer waste whenever possible.

23 24 25 26 27 28 29   7 6 5 4 3 2 1

I dedicate this book to my Lord and Savior, Jesus Christ.

Following You always leads to being uncommon.

Thank you to my beautiful wife, Linda.

You always bring out the best in me, and I look forward to many more laughs together. I love you with my whole heart.

To my four amazing children:

Michelle, who is faithful and true. I appreciate all your years of sacrifice and service to others and to me. Keep singing!

Greg, who is a man of faith and the Word and dependably supports me in prayer. We all love your sense of humor too. Keep golfing!

Mike, who is the most resourceful person I know and can build or fix anything while never missing whatever is going on around him. Keep worshiping!

Dave, who is the most competitive person I know and brings joy and passion while being the best basketball trainer anywhere. Keep helping others improve!

To my five wonderful grandchildren:

Emma, you are a tender, artistic, and sensitive girl who has your grandpa's fun-loving trickiness. Keep singing!

Olivia, you are C.E.O.livia! A loving girl and a born leader who loves to fish with Grandpa. Keep making it happen!

Beckett, you are one smart boy who can excel at so many things and loves to watch funny videos with Grandpa. Keep learning!

Darby, you are a girl full of boundless energy and smarts, and you're sure to be a great athlete someday. Keep running!

Briggs, you are a peaceful, happy baby and a joy to everyone. Keep being yourself!

To my two daughters-in-law, Brittany and Kelley:

Brittany, you are a wonderful mother and wife while excelling at your work. Keep singing and cooking!

Kelley, you are a wonderful mother and wife while juggling three little ones and staying full of faith about everything you do. Keep believing God!

Thank you, Mom and Dad.

Dad, I sure miss you, but I will see you again someday. *Mom*, thank you for your love and support all my life.

Contents

Looking Outward

Looking Upward

Contents

Acknowledgments

I want to acknowledge and offer my deepest appreciation to Baker Publishing Group and its fantastic team. A special thank-you to:

Rachel McRae, for believing in me and this book. Your leadership and guidance are much appreciated.

Amy Ballor, you have done a fantastic job editing this manuscript. I appreciate your candor and commitment to excellence.

Erin Bartels, I appreciate your writing skills and how you skillfully combine marketing and content.

Olivia Peitsch, thank you for all you do to help market the book.

Kate Guichelaar, thank you for making my books available around the world.

Eileen Hanson, I appreciate everything you do to sell my books everywhere you can.

Laura Klynstra, thank you for the beautiful cover.

Finally, to the leadership at Baker Publishing, a heartfelt thank-you for nearly twenty years of publishing my books. I appreciate you working with me to publish books that encourage people worldwide.

Introduction

I eat berries and Greek yogurt every morning, but I put them in the freezer before I do. I drink a cup of coffee daily, but I microwave it right after it's brewed. I like to think this means I have an attitude like God's. He says in Revelation 3, "I know you well—you are neither hot nor cold; I wish you were one or the other! But since you are merely lukewarm, I will spit you out of my mouth!" (vv. 15–16 TLB). I get it. I don't like lukewarm, or common, anything.

Definitions of *common* include "having no special distinction or quality" and "average or ordinary."[1] Yet God describes you and me as fearfully and wonderfully made (Ps. 139:14), as created for good works (Eph. 2:10), and as creations that put a smile on His face when He made us (1 Cor. 12:18). So there's nothing common about you. In fact, God has planned for you to be not common but uncommon.

The purpose behind everything I've written and included in this book is to attack mediocrity and show you how God wants to bring you direction, freedom, and encouragement.

Many of the personal stories I'm going to tell you happened a number of years ago. There's a reason for that. I think sometimes only the perspective of time can help us fully understand what God was doing in those earlier moments.

It's fascinating to see how God finds a way to turn what looks bad into something good and how today He's at work in our future. He has uncommon plans for you and has custom-created you to fulfill them.

As I share my personal thoughts and stories, I hope you will see how to avoid trouble, receive encouragement from the blessings He brought me, and, more importantly, understand how God's love and plan for you are blessed.

What's wonderful about God is that He can change anything in your life for good. So as you read this book, be ready to choose God's best for you. His desire is for you to *be uncommon*.

Looking

Inward

CHAPTER 1

Uncommon You

One day during the late 1980s, I was up early reading the morning paper, the *Tulsa World*. It was a daily ritual I'm sure I learned from my dad. (Nowadays, if you see someone reading an actual, physical newspaper, it's almost certain they're over forty.)

This day an article from the Associated Press caught my eye. The report stated, "Here's the average American," then described the "average" American in some detail. This American made *x* number of dollars a year. I thought, *That's what I'm making.*

Then it said this American lived in this kind of house worth *x*. *Hey, that's how much my house is worth.*

The average American also had two children. Yes, we had two kids at that time (four now). *Wow, this is getting interesting,* I thought.

The article went on to say that the most common name for a man was . . . wait for it . . . John! And the most common name for a woman was . . . drumroll . . . Linda! *Yes, that's my wife's name!*

I was amazed. I didn't know what to think. *Is this good? Or not so good?* Then I got a little upset—then a bit more upset. I had just been declared the most average person in America. At least that's how it felt.

I said out loud, "I'm not average! And you're not going to tell me I am." *I don't care what the numbers say, or what a respected news organization says, or what anyone says*, I thought resolutely. *I am not average. God fearfully and wonderfully made me unique.*

At that moment, the seeds for my first book, *An Enemy Called Average*, were planted. After that, my passion for telling others that they, too, are not average rose inside me. That passion is greater today. That's why I've written this book, *Be Uncommon*.

No matter what the "facts" may say, never let others tell you you're average or common. On the contrary, you are a genuine, one-of-a-kind, break-the-mold person. You are unique. No one in history or in the days to come will be like you.

I once read something like this: "You may not think that the world needs you, but it does. God planned it that way. No one can speak with your voice, say your words, smile your smile, or shine your light. No one can take your place, for it is yours alone to fill. If you are not here to shine your light, who knows how many other people will lose their way as they pass by your empty place in the world. You can brighten the world by leaving a little of your sparkle everywhere you go."

Stand out; don't blend in.

People connected to you are waiting to be impacted by you. You may be the answer to their prayer, a solution to their problem, an answer to their question.

Out of one hundred billion galaxies and one hundred billion star systems, you're one of the nearly eight billion people on the earth as I write this book. You have your own genetic makeup, and your blue, brown, gray, amber, hazel, green, or red irises are like none other. You are as unique as every cloud formation in the sky and every falling snowflake. Being this unique is so much better than being perfect.

Someone will always be more intelligent. Someone will always be younger. Someone will always have more money. Someone will always have more talent. Someone will always be better-looking. But no one can be or will be you.

There's a pull to get us to settle for less, to conform, to be or do like everyone else—to be common. But nothing could be further from God's plan for us. His dream for each of us is an uncommon life that glorifies Him.

Be yourself. P. T. Barnum once said, "No one ever made a difference being like everybody else." Live the story that no one else can live—the story of your own uncommon life.

CHAPTER 2

Be Grateful Always

I f you can't be satisfied with what you've reached, at least be thankful for what you've escaped.

I like to go away to write. I usually stay in some warm resort-type place and work for many days straight, barely coming out of my room unless it's to go fishing. One time, though, I decided to stay at a nice hotel in my hometown.

One evening I headed out to dinner, and as I drove I was utterly absorbed in thoughts about my latest book—so focused that I ran right through a red light at one of the busiest intersections in my city!

I was jarred out of thinking about my book when I was greeted by several horns and one man who wanted to tell me I was "number one" with his finger. Shaken, I pulled into a parking lot to give thanks to God for His protection—even when I'm stupid. Sometimes we need to be thankful for what we didn't get.

We all have much to be grateful for! Somewhere, someone is praying for something you take for granted. Be grateful for what you have. Start with thankful thoughts.

Gratitude positions us rightly before God. Therefore, how grateful you are is a sure indicator of your spiritual health. The more appreciation you have, the healthier you are.

Gratitude reveals the depth of our relationship with God. Therefore, I try to say "Thank You" to God more often than I pray "Lord, can You?" Mental health therapist Kelli Bachara once said, "If you really want to kick Satan in the teeth, immerse yourself in gratitude. Find gratitude in the tiny mundane things in your life. A sunrise. A great cup of coffee. The sound of laughter, anything, and everything. Gratitude is a powerful weapon against the one who wants to steal our joy."

Thankfulness has an incredible capacity to simplify our lives. It brings a clear, concise perspective.

You will find yourself more full of hope when you view life through the lens of gratitude.

CHAPTER 3

Character Counts

In my thirties, I worked for an organization whose owner said he had a doctorate. It was made clear to every employee how important it was to address him as Dr. _____. But it wasn't long before I decided to investigate his degree.

One day I saw a framed document in a neglected part of his office that decreed his PhD. It was for a discipline I was unfamiliar with, from a university I'd never heard of. Upon further research, I discovered the "university" was a business he'd started several years earlier. He was "conferring" master's and doctorate degrees upon ministry and business associates for a fee. In other words, he sold degrees and had given a "doctorate" *to himself*!

What a joke. Integrity is one thing for which there are no known substitutes.

The next day (I couldn't help myself), I asked some other employees if they knew where he got his doctorate and for what discipline. They didn't, and it gave me a slight, wry joy to tell them, "He got it from himself. He gave himself a doctorate!"

Then I took it a step further. I declared to as many people as I could that I was also giving a doctorate to myself. From that day forward, most of the people who worked at that organization referred to me as "Doc"—and still do!

One other humorous side story about this . . .

Later that year, I stopped a book from going to press because the cover said "Foreword by Dr. John Mason." So I guess some people thought I genuinely had a doctorate—or at least that I'd bought one.

Be honest with God, others, those you're closest to, and yourself. Christianity is not about hiding and deception.

You are what you do, not what you promise to do. If the words don't add up, it's usually because an exemplary character wasn't included in the equation. I respect and rely on people who have proven character. Run the race with a team that values integrity.

There's no limit to the height you can attain by remaining on the level. Integrity is still the best policy. Today, however, there are fewer policyholders than there used to be. Warren Buffett said, "In looking for people to hire, you look for three qualities: integrity, intelligence, and energy. And if they don't have the first, the other two will kill you."

Having character will win every argument if you stick with it long enough. Integrity may not be popular, but it's always right. The fact that nobody else around you wants to do what's right should never stop you. Proverbs 28:6 tells us, "Better is a poor man who walks in his integrity than a rich man who is crooked in his ways" (ESV).

Have character in the dark and be humble in the light. It may seem that compromising your character will take care of the present, but it has no future. Know what's right and do what's right. If something you've done costs you your character, you paid too much.

CHAPTER 4

Stay Off the Slippery Slope

While attending college, I became friends with a fellow student who was the university's men's basketball team manager. I'll never forget the day he asked me one of the most random questions I'd ever been asked.

Out of the blue, he said, "John, how would you like to be the Harlem Globetrotters' basketball team manager?" Of course, I thought he was joking, but he went on to say that the team had selected our campus as their home base during breaks in their travels, and he'd been filling the role of manager for them for the past couple of years. But he no longer planned to do it.

Now the team had asked him if he knew anyone who could take his place. So, for the next several years, they planned to spend several weeks on campus practicing, and at the end of each year, they would host a game there for the city of Tulsa.

Well, it didn't take me long to say, "Absolutely yes!" Not only had I heard of the Harlem Globetrotters, but I'd even attended a couple of their games. They put on a great show.

The team hired me. I remember heading out to the campus arena where they practiced and walking into the locker room for the first time. There in front of me stood internationally known players Curly Neal, Bobby Joe Mason (no relation to me), and the most famous Globetrotter of all, Meadowlark Lemon. Meadowlark played in more than sixteen thousand games as a Globetrotter and was a 2003 inductee into the Naismith Memorial Basketball Hall of Fame. I was surprised when they warmly received me as their manager.

Right away, I jumped into my managerial chores: making sure all the basketballs were available, water cups were filled, and, of course, all their props were ready. Props such as the basketball attached to a rubber band that sprang back when passed to somebody, the bucket they carried to throw confetti on people who anticipated water instead, and the weighted basketballs that wouldn't bounce. It was fascinating and surreal to hold those world-famous items in my hands.

They gave me handfuls of tickets for free. Back then, every game was a sellout, so it meant a lot to me when one of their stars, Curly Neal, said, "Here, John. Go sell these and do something nice for your girlfriend" (Linda, who later became my wife). Although this team was full of world-famous celebrities, the players were still regular guys who remembered what it was like to be a young college student.

As the manager, I had to do their laundry, which I didn't particularly enjoy. But while doing it, I encountered one of my most memorable temptations.

Bobby Joe Mason was one of their stars, and I was responsible for washing his game jersey. The Harlem Globetrotters' uniforms are recognizable worldwide to any basketball fan: red and white stripes on a dark-blue background with prominent white stars and the name Harlem Globetrotters emblazoned across the front. Bobby Joe's jersey was especially impressive and enticing to me because the name MASON was embroidered on the back of the uniform across the shoulders.

Nobody was around. No one would see. *Wow, wouldn't I look great wearing that jersey?* I thought—just for a moment. Then I came to my senses. *There's no way I'm going to steal this jersey.* Looking back, I think if I'd only asked Bobby Joe, he probably would have given me his jersey since each player had other, identical ones. But do you think I would have enjoyed wearing that jersey knowing I would be reminded how I got it every time I did?

Sin grows best in the dark, out of sight, when you're by yourself. The good news is you don't have to fight this battle alone. God is with you, by your side, to show you the way out. Though temptation is everywhere, remember that God is everywhere too. Kelli Mahoney says, "To overcome temptation, you must identify what leads you away from God."

First Corinthians 10:13 tells us, "The temptations in your life are no different from what others experience. And God is faithful. He will not allow the temptation to be more than you can stand. When you are tempted, he will show you a way out so that you can endure" (NLT).

Romans 12:21 says, "Do not be overcome by evil, but overcome evil with good." Your right, godly decisions make a difference. Making them is one of the surest ways to fight this battle. Decide to say no. Sin is easier to say no to today than tomorrow. In her book *Making Good Habits, Breaking Bad Habits*, Joyce Meyer writes, "If we are not actively doing what is right, it becomes very easy for the devil to get us to do what is wrong."[1]

Remember the saying "If you don't want temptation to follow you, don't act as if you're interested"? Matthew 26:41 tells us to instead "watch and pray so that you will not fall into temptation. The spirit is willing, but the flesh is weak." When faced with the opportunity to sin, ask yourself, *Is what I'm about to do worth losing what I have?*

As a young man, I was privileged to have dinner with Ezra Taft Benson and his wife, Flora, in Washington, DC. Ezra was the former Secretary of Agriculture under President Eisenhower and was known for his powerful saying about temptation: "It is easier to prepare and prevent than to repair and repent." So decide during the day how you will act in the darkness of night when temptation comes knocking.

Someone once declared, "You can't defeat the demons you enjoy playing with." Temptation usually walks through a door that was intentionally left open. Slam those doors shut. Say no!

One of the main reasons many people don't make it to the finish line is that they keep stopping for temptation. Here's the way to avoid those detours:

Let God work his will in you. Yell a loud no to the Devil and watch him make himself scarce. Say a quiet yes to God and he'll be there in no time. Quit dabbling in sin. Purify your inner life. Quit playing the field. Hit bottom, and cry your eyes out. The fun and games are over. Get serious, really serious. Get down on your knees before the Master; it's the only way you'll get on your feet. (James 4:7–10 MSG)

CHAPTER 5

Do Good, Choose Right

Sheltering at home in the middle of a pandemic will mess with your mind.

While out for a daily walk in the neighborhood with my wife, I spotted a twenty-dollar bill on the grass between the sidewalk and the street. I'm thinking, *Outback steak! Delivered to my house!* But Linda said, "Stop! Don't touch that! Don't pick it up!"

So, of course, I picked it up, thinking I'd just go straight back to our house to wash my hands for twenty seconds. Filthy lucre!

We looked up and down the street to see if someone was looking for money the Oklahoma wind had blown from their hand. In the end, Linda had the best idea. She suggested we give the twenty bucks to the high school graduate whose house had a sign celebrating her—the home with the yard where we found the cash. So we rang the doorbell, but no one answered. Of course, I'd hoped they would tell us to just keep it.

We walked back home, found a graduation greeting card, wrote a congratulatory note to the graduate, and enclosed the twenty-dollar gift. When we returned to the neighbor's house a little while later, we laid the card on the doormat and then rang the doorbell again. This time a man answered, and from more than six feet away, we told him the story of finding the twenty dollars near the curb in front of his house and deciding to give it to the graduate, who, as it turned out, was his daughter.

He picked up the card and told us, "I'm so glad you're telling me this. One of my workers collected some rent money for me, and when I went to deposit it at the bank, the amount was twenty dollars short. I couldn't figure out what happened." He good-naturedly laughed about the outcome!

So what is the lesson? Is it to always do what your wife says? Probably. But I think more importantly, whether good or bad fortune comes your way, responding the right way will always lead to good results. You may not personally receive the positive effect, but your response is sure to be a blessing to someone else. Be the reason someone feels accepted, noticed, appreciated, heard, and loved.

Saying something good to others isn't always the easiest thing to say. In fact, the five hardest things to say are:

1. I love you.
2. I was wrong, and I'm sorry.
3. I need help.
4. I appreciate you.
5. Worcestershire sauce.
    (Just kidding on the last one.)

Somebody somewhere still remembers you today because you were good to them when no one else was. The world says to take care of yourself, but God says to take care of others and He will take care of you.

Do good for others. It will come back in unexpected ways. The Bible promises that the good things you make happen for others, God will make happen for you: "Knowing that whatever good anyone does, he will receive the same from the Lord" (Eph. 6:8 NKJV).

Don't be concerned about whether anybody will see your good deeds. The sun rises beautifully in the morning while most of us are asleep. Several people have been quoted saying, "Do everything with a good heart and expect nothing in return, and you will never be disappointed." Understand that sometimes others don't notice the good things we do for them until we stop doing them. Do not allow the actions or inactions of others to decrease your efforts to do good.

You will never regret being kind. If you find yourself in a place to change a negative atmosphere to a positive one, do it. The world needs more of that. Be a hope giver, because once you offer hope, you make anything possible. A positive word brightens a dark world. Focusing on the good has a way of driving out a lot of what's bad. So bring a little sunshine everywhere you go.

CHAPTER 6

No Matter How Long You've Traveled in the Wrong Direction, You Can Still Turn Around

Awhile back, it was trendy for families to hang a yellow, diamond-shaped sign that said Baby on Board on the rear windows of their cars. You could find these signs in minivans and SUVs all over America.

I purchased a yellow sign like that as well, but mine said Stunt Driver. I must admit that sign made me laugh, and friends who saw it got a chuckle out of it too. But all the laughter stopped one day on my way home from work.

I left my office right at rush hour and was trying to merge onto a busy highway that was one-way from my left to the right.

So I was looking to my left, looking for the best time to pull out into traffic. I'd done this on hundreds of occasions, usually at the same time of day with the same busyness. I would ease my way onto the highway safely and then head home for dinner.

This day seemed like any other as I patiently waited for a chance to pull out. Then, finally, I saw an opening and had just begun to merge onto the highway when I heard a big thump on the right side of my car!

I immediately pulled to the side of the road, stopped, and looked into my rearview mirror, only to see a man sprawled out in the middle of the pavement with a bicycle lying beside him.

I cautiously pulled off onto a side street. The first thing that came to mind (I'm embarrassed to say) wasn't how I was going to help this person. It was *Oh no! I've just collided with somebody, and I have a Stunt Driver sign in my back window!*

I scrambled to the back seat of my car, reached up, and tore the sign from my window. I didn't want anyone, especially a police officer, to think I thought I was a stunt driver. I got out of my car, and by the time I got to the person lying in the street, a lady was already there praying over him.

He'd been biking the wrong way on a one-way street. As I pulled out, he ran into my car bumper, flew over the top of my car, and landed on the road, instantly breaking his leg. He was obviously in a lot of pain, and I felt very sorry for him.

The police arrived in a matter of minutes. I'll never forget an officer coming over, listening to me talk about what happened, and then saying, "I guess he learned his lesson. Going down a one-way street the wrong way is a formula for disaster."

Speeding along the wrong way may work for a while—even for a long time. But eventually, something bad will probably happen. What benefit is running if you're on the wrong road?

Simon Sinek once commented that "it is better to go slow in the right direction than to go fast in the wrong direction." There's nothing wrong with change if it's in the right direction. Others have been quoted saying, "It is better to walk alone than with a crowd going in the wrong direction." Stop chasing the wrong path.

Many times, the action you take at the right time has no immediate impact on the end result, but it gets you to the right place at the right time, going in the right direction.

Be careful about rushing God's timing and changing His direction. You never know who or what He's protecting you from or leading you to.

Nothing good happens when we choose to go the wrong way, especially when the right path is in the opposite direction. I wonder if the man who crashed into my car had biked the wrong direction many times with no issues. But one day he encountered an obstacle (my car) that stopped him. I guarantee that when he could get back on his bike, he never went down that one-way street the wrong way again.

CHAPTER 7

Finish First, Quit Last

Never give up on what you know you should do. I've observed that about 97 percent of the people who stopped too soon are employed by the 3 percent who never gave up. Many of the world's great failures did not realize how close they were to success when they gave up. Your success begins where most others quit.

Galatians 6:9 says, "Let us not become weary in doing good, for at the proper time we will reap a harvest if we do not give up." Is it that simple? Yes!

Here's my challenge to you today: become famous for completing important, challenging tasks. I promise you will be shocked at the impact of your persistence.

More than thirty years ago, I felt led to write a book, but I knew more than a thousand new books were published each day and that most of them were read by very few people.

When I was in college, if you had asked me to list fifty things I would do, writing a book wouldn't have been one of them. But I started and worked at it for nearly two years. I had no As in English let alone a built-in audience, but I did have the determination and a commitment to finish. I'll never forget typing the last word into my Apple IIc computer (with only 128K of memory) at 4:30 in the morning, then falling into my bed and sobbing for quite a while. It was finished!

The book was *An Enemy Called Average*. Little did I know that more than seven hundred thousand people would read this book in nearly forty languages around the world.

Recently, I was pondering how good God has been to me about the sales of that book. I was blown away when I realized that if one copy of all the copies sold was laid on the equator at every mile, they could encircle the earth twenty-four times. Wow! God is good, and He sure does have "the whole world in His hands."

Again, you will be shocked at the impact of your persistence!

Be thankful for your challenge; you might not have discovered your strength without it. Difficult roads often lead to beautiful destinations. Winston Churchill said, "Never give up on something that you can't go a day without thinking about."

Coca-Cola sold only twenty-five bottles in its first year. Every start-up begins with zero customers, zero sales, and zero profits.

The sure way to succeed is to never give up. And never give up without a fight. Giving up on your goal because of one setback is like throwing away three good tires because a fourth tire went flat.

Luke 18:1 says to "always pray and never give up" (NLT). Every time you feel like quitting, consider why you began. Be relentless in the pursuit of what sets your heart on fire.

"It's impossible," said Pride.

"It's risky," said Experience.

"It's pointless," said Reason.

"Give it a try," whispered the heart.

Stop waiting to do the things you want to do. Today is the day to just go for it. Hebrews 12:1–3 in The Message says, "We'd better get on with it. Strip down, start running—and never quit! No extra spiritual fat, no parasitic sins. Keep your eyes on *Jesus*, who both began and finished this race we're in. Study how he did it. Because he never lost sight of where he was headed—that exhilarating finish in and with God."

The moment you're ready to quit is usually the moment right before a breakthrough happens. So don't give up!

Souls are attached to your gifts and calling. Your persistence impacts others. Someday in the future, people will thank you because you didn't give up today. Your breakthrough is never just about you; it's also about the people who will be blessed and encouraged because you didn't quit.

CHAPTER 8

You Can Be Humble and Strong at the Same Time

We don't always get what we want, but let's humbly consider this: some people will never have what we have right now.

Some time ago, I went to a Mexican fast-food restaurant. As I stood in line for service, I noticed an elderly lady in front of me who seemed to be a destitute street person. I concluded that about her because she was carrying a grocery bag filled to the top with what looked like all her possessions in the world. When it was her turn, she ordered some water and one taco.

Sitting in the booth right next to her, I couldn't help but observe her and be moved with compassion for her. Shortly after I began my meal, I walked over and asked if I could buy more food for her lunch.

She looked at me and angrily asked, "Who are you?"

"Just a guy who wants to help," I responded.

She ignored me.

I finished my meal about the same time she did, and we both got up to leave. I followed her out of the restaurant because I felt led to give her some money. So in the parking lot, I approached her and offered her some cash.

Her only response was, "Stop bothering me!" Then she stormed off.

Immediately, the Lord spoke this to my heart: "That's the way My people respond to Me. I'm up in heaven wanting to pour out a blessing, and they respond, 'Who are You? What do You want from me?' They don't realize it's Me trying to bless their lives!"

Being the gracious God that He is, the Lord continues to try to bless us. But we react by saying, "Stop bothering me." Missing out on the rich blessings of the Lord, we walk away, just as this lady walked away from me. Imagine what would have happened if she had humbled herself and accepted what God, through me, was offering. Instead of rejecting God's help, we should be humble and receive whatever He has for us however He chooses to bring it to us.

The Bible tells us that when we are weak, God makes us strong (2 Cor. 12:10). So by God's grace, be strong when you're weak. Brave when you're scared. Humble when you're victorious. Preacher Jonathan Edwards noted that "nothing sets a person so much out of the devil's reach as humility."

Ephesians 4:2 says, "Be completely humble and gentle; be patient, bearing with one another in love." Not everything you do needs to be seen or told.

No one is more unstoppable than a humble person with a tenacious spirit guided by a divine purpose. So do as Jim Rohn charged: "Be strong, but not rude; be kind, but not weak; be bold, but not a bully; be thoughtful, but not lazy; be humble, but not timid; be proud, but not arrogant."

CHAPTER 9

Nothing Changes If Nothing Changes

It was a brilliant day, and I was panicking.

Having just left church, I'd wandered from the dark, air-conditioned auditorium into the bright noonday sun. My eyes scanned the vast parking lot filled with several thousand cars looking for my own, but it was nowhere to be found. I thought my old Chevrolet Caprice Classic—broken front seat and all—had been stolen at church!

Strangely, I had an epiphany. My thoughts flowed from fear to fortune as I thought, *Maybe it's really gone, and I can get some much-needed insurance money for that old clunker.*

With each passing moment, I felt happier and happier with my newfound "miracle"—until I unexpectedly and disappointingly found my car parked right where I'd left it, hidden between two Oklahoma-sized pickup trucks.

What was I actually looking for once I thought my car had been stolen? Change. You might say I was looking for change in all the wrong places. So many of us do that. We want others to change, circumstances to change, our location or job to change. Yet this is the time for you and me to fully embrace the people God created us to be.

Author John Mark Green observes, "Change. It can be hard. It requires no extra effort to settle for the same old thing. Auto-pilot keeps us locked into past patterns. But transforming your life? That requires courage, commitment, and effort. It's tempting to stay camped in the zone of That's-Just-How-It-Is. But to get to the really good stuff in life, you have to be willing to become an explorer and adventurer."

Making a life change is pretty scary. But you know what's even scarier? Regret. Take advantage of change and make the most of the opportunity it presents.

As you change, don't be afraid of what could go wrong. Instead, focus your thoughts on what could go right. Change is not a painful ending—it's a new beginning. You're about to meet the real you!

Playing it safe is probably the most unsafe thing in the world. You cannot stand still. You must go forward and be open to those adjustments that improve you. Seize the way!

Focus your energy not on recapturing the old but on building the new. Save yourself some heartache and pain—stop looking for happiness where you lost it. The most hazardous thought you can have is, *I've always done it this way.*

Things change. When we were kids, we were told not to get into cars with strangers. Then we were told never to meet alone with someone we know only from the internet. Now we're told to contact Uber, order ourselves a stranger, and get into

41

their car alone with them so they can take us where we want to go.

Life changes, and so can you. Close some doors that no longer lead to where you're supposed to be. Take the step of faith. Walk in peace through doors only God can open.

The changes I'm presenting in this book can be uncomfortable. But being uncommon never comes from the comfort zone. To be uncommon, get comfortable with being uncomfortable. And as you choose to change for the better, do your best not to consider your past mistakes.

You're not stuck with the way things are right now. Change is better than being unhappy. One choice can change everything. So make the change. Don't settle for an uncommon life.

CHAPTER 10

To Tell the Truth

Here's one of my favorite stories I heard years ago:

My teacher asked me what my favorite animal was, and I said, "Fried chicken." She told me that wasn't funny, but she couldn't have been right because everyone else laughed.

My parents always told me to tell the truth, so I did. Fried chicken is my favorite animal! I told my dad what happened, and he said my teacher was probably a member of PETA. He said they love animals very much. I do too. Especially chicken, pork, and beef.

Anyway, my teacher sent me to the principal's office. I told him what happened, and he laughed too. Then he told me not to do it again.

The next day in class, my teacher asked me what my favorite live animal was. I told her it was a chicken. She asked me why, so I told her it was because you can make them into fried chicken.

She sent me back to the principal's office. He laughed again and said not to do it again.

I didn't understand. My parents taught me to be honest, but my teacher didn't like it when I was. The next day, she asked me what famous person I admired most.

I told her, "Colonel Sanders." Guess where I was headed?

Honesty will take you places you want to be and sometimes places you may not want to be. But where you land will always be better than if you're dishonest.

I don't want to be around people who don't understand the concept of accuracy as honesty. They say, "If by faith I believe it will happen, it's OK to go ahead and say it." *Really?* I thought when I heard this from a man I'll call Sam, a senior executive. He believed he could say anything was true whether or not it actually was—if by faith he believed it *would* happen.

He then proceeded to claim that sales were higher than they were and that profits were increasing when, instead, the company was on the edge of bankruptcy. Finally, he proclaimed that new deals were imminent when they were far into the future. He sincerely believed all these statements *would* come true. He was speaking in what he called faith. But what he said wasn't happening at the time. It simply wasn't true.

I've heard it said that the truth doesn't cost you anything, but a lie could cost you everything. Eventually, it all came crashing down for this executive and his company. Hope built on a lie always leads to loss.

Truth exists. Lies must be made up. Painter Georges Braque said, "Only falsehood has to be invented."

God doesn't need our help, our "faith talk," to prop up what He's doing. The truth is more than enough. Is it OK to "evangelistically" speak about events or numbers? Are we to "top that testimony" if we get the chance? No, never fall into that trap.

Just be honest with me—or go away. I respect people with sincere intentions who tell me the truth every time. I can depend on and work with honest people.

The truth has no legitimate alternatives. There is no acceptable substitute for honesty and no valid excuse for dishonesty.

"If you tell the truth, your problem becomes part of your past. If you lie, it becomes part of your future," said basketball coach Rick Pitino. So, choose honesty, and you'll find freedom in your future. You won't have to live looking over your shoulder for any untruths trying to catch up to you.

Truth outlives a lie. Proverbs 12:19 tells us, "Truthful lips endure forever, but a lying tongue lasts only a moment."

We all know that honesty is the best policy, but what are the benefits of that policy?

Living honestly

- reduces stress because you don't have to remember what you said and live up to unattainable expectations.
- allows you to genuinely care for others because you are truthful in your feelings.
- offers safety in relationships because you're surrounded by people who accept you as you are.
- simplifies your life from overpromising and unrealistic expectations.
- opens you to provide trustworthy advice for others and yourself.
- frees you to be yourself and no longer pretend to be somebody else to gain acceptance from others.

- increases your value. When people can depend on your words and actions, they want to work and associate with you.
- improves focus because you're not distracted by untrue statements and commitments.
- creates long-lasting relationships because trust is the centerpiece of your associations.
- reduces guilt and shame. You may fool others, but *you* will always know what is true or false.
- provides a more direct path to answers you're seeking and goals you want to achieve. Lies lead to nowhere. Shortcuts cost you more than they appear to save you.
- gives you more energy because dishonesty takes a lot of effort to keep the pretense going.
- creates opportunity. Who would you rather do business with or spend time with—an honest or a dishonest person?
- attracts other honest people and replaces dishonest people in your life. According to my friend Pastor David Blunt, "If you continue to do what's right, what's wrong and who's wrong will eventually leave your life."
- keeps you out of trouble. You do reap what you sow. Your words and actions are seeds that bring forth good fruit or bad.
- gives you better health mentally and physically.[1]
- increases courage. Standing for the truth is not always easy, but it is always right.
- sometimes causes short-term pain, but truth provides long-term gain.

- gives you consistency. Remain on the level and you won't have so many highs and lows. Life is uncertain enough without your help.
- releases and frees you to run with your dreams. It is true that "you will know the truth, and the truth will set you free" (John 8:32 NASB).

Why was Abraham Lincoln known as Honest Abe? As a young boy working in a small-town store, Lincoln would walk however far he needed to repay a customer whenever he accidentally overcharged them. By doing this, he became known as Honest Abe. Leonard Swett, one of the president's closest friends, said this of the former president: "He believed in the great laws of truth, the right discharge of duty, his accountability to God, the ultimate triumph of the right, and the overthrow of wrong." You can learn from Lincoln's principles and determine to live an honest life, and perhaps you can be known as "Honest _____."

CHAPTER 11

Where You Are Is the Best Place to Start

The phone rang in my office. When I answered, a pastor identified himself, then said, "I've heard about the consulting work you do with churches. I'd like to fly you up to Minneapolis to interview you about using your services and have you give your opinion about an issue that's before our board right now."

"Of course," I responded. "I'd be honored to come and meet with you and your board. And hopefully to be able to consult your church in the future."

I wanted to say more, but the pastor interrupted me by asking, "Do you preach too?" I hesitated. I hadn't preached yet, but the Lord had been leading me to start preaching. So I said, "Yes, I preach."

"Fine. I want you to preach in both the Sunday morning and Sunday evening services. But we're a small inner-city church, so I can give you only one hundred dollars." I said yes. I was now committed, surprised, and a little nervous.

I flew into the Twin Cities, and the pastor met me at the airport in a full-length mink coat! We went from baggage claim straight to his car, a new BMW 7 Series. I was thinking, *Something is wrong with this picture*. Little did I know this might be foreshadowing of something else being wrong.

He took me to the church briefly before heading to my hotel. The church was downtown and looked to have a seating capacity of only about two hundred. So again, I wondered about the pastor's expensive coat and car. But once checked into my hotel, I focused on preparing for the next day's meetings and messages.

This was my very first time preaching, and I awoke the next morning with an excitement I'd never experienced. I was looking forward to sharing with this man's congregation.

Like most services, this one began with singing, congregants sharing announcements, and prayer requests. Then it was time for the sermon, and the pastor eloquently introduced me.

I rose from my seat in the front row.

Bounded up the steps toward the pulpit.

And fell flat on my face when I missed the last step!

What a way to launch my preaching career! I gathered myself, walked behind the pulpit, and said, "Now that I have your attention . . ." and began my message.

I gave it my all, and the people responded well. Then as I was closing, I sensed in my heart that I should invite people to come to the altar for prayer. So I did.

I prayed for each person who came, and I was almost finished when a young man with his head bowed looked up and asked for prayer. As soon as I began to pray for him, I strongly felt I should also pray for his family—specifically for his relationship with his father. So I did—out loud.

Shortly afterward I learned his father was the pastor who had invited me to speak! He was rather upset with my public prayer for his son, and again I felt like, *What a start!*

After the service, I met with the pastor in his office, where he told me I was no longer invited to speak at the evening service because of my prayer. Then the situation worsened when he told me he wanted me to present to the board an endorsement for an idea I knew was clearly unethical. I'm sure he knew it wasn't right too. Obviously, he'd brought me in to give his lousy idea credibility.

I refused to do it.

I don't remember if he gave me the hundred dollars. He probably did. But what is most interesting is what happened next. He abandoned the church and his wife for another woman three weeks later, leaving his wife to pastor the church alone.

About fifteen years after this experience, I spoke at a pastors' conference. A nice young man came up to me at the break and asked if I recognized him. I told him, "I'm sorry, I don't."

"You prayed for me at my father's church years ago," he said. "God used you that day." After I understood who he was, he went on. "My situation was bad, but I knew I couldn't tell anyone. My mom is doing well leading the church. I'm now married, volunteering at the church, and I have a young child. We're all serving the Lord!"

Don't judge how you *start* on God's path for you as an indication of how well (or not so well) it will go. You might get out of the gate like the racehorse Secretariat, or you might fall flat on your face. Either way, the only option to go forward is to be submitted to God's will, to be committed to serving others, and to always tell the truth. *Just begin*, and you will find yourself halfway there. Every destiny requires a first step.

The Bible reminds us not to despise the day of small beginnings (Zech. 4:10). Or as Pat Robertson once shared, "Despise not the day of small beginnings because you can make all your mistakes anonymously."

In his book *On Writing*, author Stephen King writes, "The scariest moment is always just before you start."[1] I've heard many times that "if you don't go after what you want, you'll never have it. If you don't ask, the answer will always be no. If you don't step forward, you will always be in the same place."

Where should you go? The Bible tells us, "Your word is a lamp to my feet and a light to my path" (Ps. 119:105 NKJV). God's Holy Scriptures will guide you now (a lamp to your feet) and in the future (a light to your path). God says, "I will instruct you and teach you in the way you should go; I will guide you with My eye" (Ps. 32:8 NKJV). You are God's number one thought. His eye is on you. Let Him show you the way.

Blogger and CEO Naeem Callaway once said, "Sometimes the smallest step in the right direction ends up being the biggest step of your life. Tiptoe if you must, but take the step."

Right where you are is the best place to start. Big things often have small beginnings. Discover the value of going forward—take that first step!

Faith takes the first step even when you can't see the whole staircase. Determine to take a small action every day. Big wins start as small steps. Your greatest successes will be found one step at a time.

What small step can you take right now? My beginning mistakes are not so anonymous now because of some of the books I've written. But I wouldn't trade those experiences and lessons for anything. So as you move forward, know that God looks at your heart, not your eloquence—nor at your ability to climb the steps without falling.

CHAPTER 12

Different Is the Difference

I wasn't concerned about whether I was different; I was concerned about whether I was the same as everyone else.

When I wrote my first book, I knew I needed to make it stand out and not blend in. Yet as an unknown author with no platform or previous bookselling history, I faced an uphill battle in making my book known to the masses.

Since I was experienced in publishing, I should have had an advantage. But I was unsure what that advantage was exactly.

I've always hated having to read twenty pages to get one point. I know some people enjoy being drawn into the beautiful details of illustrious writing, but I find it boring. I'm impatient.

So I decided to do something no one else was doing at the time—write two-page chapters. That was about how long my interest held, and I figured that was true for many others too. People could read four chapters and feel very proud even though they'd read only eight pages! Plus, it forced me to make every word count. I remember trying to make each sentence stand on its own.

Hundreds of people have told me they bought my books because of the short chapters. Probably the most hilarious comment I get is people telling me they read my books in their bathroom! An embarrassed smile usually follows, from both them and me. I often can't help but respond, "I'm not surprised. Each nugget chapter is just the right length and quite moving!"

I did a second thing in my book that was almost sacrilegious: I didn't boldface the Scripture. Authors at that time always did that to differentiate Scripture and make it stand out. But I knew many people skipped or glanced over the Scripture in books—especially lengthy passages or verses they already knew. So instead (watch out for lightning!), I chose to boldface my best one-liners. I wanted to highlight my best thoughts so as people flipped through the book in stores, they could see I offered some compelling expressions. So instead of boldfacing the Scripture passages, I decided to italicize them, still highlighting and differentiating them from my own thoughts.

Of course, I was criticized. "Your book is a mile wide and an inch deep," said one church leader. "You're elevating your thoughts above the Bible." I welcomed the critics. I was standing out, and my writing style was helping people read the book and then tell others about it.

I knew 70 percent of all books were never read, which motivated me. So I determined to write a book people *would* read! I knew that if someone actually reads a book, they're likely to tell someone else about it. Word of mouth is the best way to get your message out and sell a lot of books at the same time. It's a win-win for everyone!

Pablo Picasso said, "Learn the rules like a pro, so you can break them like an artist." To be a success, you must stand out, not blend in. You must be odd to be number one.

Break the rules more often, and you'll gain a considerable advantage over those too afraid to risk it. Take advantage of everyone's natural desire to conform. Color outside the lines.

If you don't fit in, you're probably doing the right thing. See your difference as a strength. Author Royale Scuderi notes, "Be humble enough to know you're not better than everyone else and wise enough to know that you're different from the rest." Be humble and confident at the same time.

"I want to stand as close to the edge as I can without going over. Out on the edge, you see all the kinds of things you can't see from the center," proclaims writer Kurt Vonnegut.[1]

Find your difference and embrace it. You will never influence the world by imitating it. Instead, make a deliberate choice to be different.

CHAPTER 13

Keep Swinging

If you play golf long enough, you will have your own "Tiger Woods moment."

Out to golf with a couple of friends at a local course, I played the first four holes like I usually did—a par, a bogey, another par, and one more bogey on the fourth hole. The fifth hole was one of my favorites, so I confidently grabbed my pitching wedge as I stepped up to the tee. I'd played this short par three many times before, and I knew precisely which club to use.

I set the ball on the tee, stood behind the ball, and lined up my shot. After I struck the ball, I noticed I'd hit it better than usual because it was flying straight to where I'd aimed it. As the ball arced high in the air toward the flag, I hoped I'd selected the right club to go the proper distance. The ball landed about ten feet in front of the hole, then spun forward and fell into the hole.

My first hole in one!

It didn't take me long to run to the green, let out a shout, and grab the ball from the hole. (Unfortunately, three holes later, I hit that same "miracle" ball into the water, never to be seen again. No special trophy for that ball or me. I felt like an idiot.)

Golf Digest and the National Hole in One Association estimate that a tee shot hit by an amateur golfer on a par three lands in the hole only one out of every 12,500 times.[1] My shot was now one out of those 12,500 times. On the other hand, my son Greg, a professional golfer for more than ten years, has made eight holes in one, including two on par fours.

In 1959, police were called to the Lake City Public Library in Lake City, South Carolina, when a nine-year-old African American boy trying to check out books refused to leave after being told the library was not for black people. The police told the librarian to let him check out the books anyway, and undeterred, the boy kept reading and grew up to earn a PhD in physics from MIT and receive several honorary doctorates. Ronald McNair later became an astronaut and a crew member of the ill-fated Space Shuttle Challenger. On January 29, 2011, the library that refused to lend him books was dedicated as the Ronald E. McNair Life History Center.[2]

I believe unusual positive outcomes happen if you keep doing your best over time. I'm sure if that were my first time playing golf, I would have had zero chance to hit a hole in one. I kept trying, after missing thousands of times, before that ball rolled into the hole.

If Dr. McNair had stopped reading, he never would have reached his dream of becoming an astronaut. So let us run the race that is before us and never give up. We should remove from our lives anything that could get in the way and the sin that so easily holds us back. Hebrews 12:2 says, "Let us look only to

Jesus, the One who began our faith and who makes it perfect" (NCV).

One of my favorite quotes comes from Happy Caldwell: "If you do the right thing long enough, you will become a hero simply by the process of elimination." Persistence will take you farther than intelligence.

Proverbs 28:20 states, "A faithful man will abound with blessings" (NKJV). A rock is broken with the last strike of the hammer. That doesn't mean the other strikes were worthless. The continuous and persistent effort brings results. Challenging times often bring the highest moments in your life. Keep going. Persistence can chip a boulder into a statue. Be thankful for what you have while pressing toward what you want. Keep believing and moving forward "because you know that the testing of your faith produces perseverance" (James 1:3).

As you determine to succeed, the path won't get any easier, but you will find yourself getting stronger. You're not in this alone. Keep going, and one day you'll thank yourself for being persistent. Remember the saying "No matter how slow you go, you're still lapping everyone on the couch." Persistence wins.

Nothing worthwhile comes easy. If you didn't stick with it, you probably never really wanted it. Never stop when you're down. Stop only when you're finished. Try one more time!

Keep going, my friend. The world is waiting to see what happens when you don't give up.

CHAPTER 14

True Freedom Comes from Knowing for Yourself

Proverbs 18:1 says, "One who separates himself seeks his own desire. He quarrels against all sound wisdom" (NASB). Separation and isolation lead to being an island unto yourself. Being isolated always reduces excellence because there's no competition.

Disconnect from people who want to control you. Controllers don't want you to connect with anyone else; they want you to think they have all the answers to your questions, both spiritual and personal.

In relationships, there's no such thing as one-stop shopping for all the truth. When you're isolated, it's easier to be deceived or defeated.

We faced a question many Christian parents face. Should we send our children to a Christian school or to a public school?

Linda and I grew up attending public schools. I think we both turned out all right—at least, I know Linda did.

We'd sent our first two children to a local Christian school, but now it was time for our next two to start school. We had just moved back to Tulsa after a three-year stint running a publishing company in Orlando, Florida, so we were starting over in Tulsa, where we still live.

The public schools in the school district had (and still have) a reputation for excellence, known for top academics and a great, positive, and mostly Christian environment. We also knew what we would get at the local Christian school since our two oldest children had attended there before we moved.

A pastor friend, Bill Scheer, started and currently pastors a great church in Tulsa, GUTS Church. He was at our house when we shared our two choices with him. Bill encouraged us to consider the public school. I wasn't surprised by his suggestion; Bill has always been about being a light where there's darkness. In my opinion, probably no other church in our city reaches the lost in as many arenas as his. Yet I did find it interesting, in a good way, that a pastor would recommend a public school over a Christian one.

We were determined to consider both. Since we already had experience with the Christian school—primarily good—we ventured out to the public school. Linda took the lead, interviewing teachers and administrators and asking questions.

Then on one of her visits, God decided to show us the way.

While inside the school, Linda felt strongly that the Lord wanted her to drop to her knees and dedicate our children to His glory in that school. As she did, it became clear that they should go there. So without hesitation, we enrolled them.

Not long after, during the summer break, we received a letter addressed to all the parents of students at the Christian school from the superintendent saying it was God's will for *every* student to attend *only* a Christian school. Frankly, this letter ticked me off. I thought, *How can that possibly be true? Where would you put them all?* I also thought, *He probably attended a public school growing up. What about being a light to darkness? Oh well . . .*

Thankfully, we were secure in our faith and relationship with the Lord, no matter one man's opinion. I hate it when people proclaim absolutes about something for which they should be open to God's will. I dislike it because it causes people to make wrong decisions. One size does not fit all.

To me, the letter said, "Don't think and don't discover for yourself," and though not in so many words, it also said, "Keep God out of it."

By the way, our experience at the public school was excellent. It was the very best for our kids, and we're glad we listened to and obeyed God.

The truth isn't hard to see. What's difficult is when people add to it.

No one person has all the answers. No one organization has all the answers and opportunities. Belief in one human authority is the greatest enemy of truth.

Have you heard of the Four Spiritual Laws? The foundational premise is that "God loves you, and He has a wonderful plan for your life." Have you ever found yourself feeling that another person, an organization, or a church is saying God loves you, but *they* have a wonderful plan for your life? As a result, they try to make what they do appear to be the most important and valuable, thus anything you decide to do differently to be less important and valuable. Don't let others create your world out of their need. Don't let them limit your relationship with God to theirs.

Watch out for someone or something that tries to be everything in your life. Could it be the reason they want to separate you from others is not for your benefit but because they feel threatened by those others? If you accept this, it will limit your possibilities and shrink your dream to fit within theirs. That isn't best for you or your family. One positive thing about getting a little older is that my eyesight might be weaker, but I can see through people much better.

If someone says they have all the answers for everything, watch out! It's good to have people in your life who say, "I don't know." On the other hand, it's bizarre for people to think they know everything.

The truth is leaders and organizations that feel they always know what's best for you don't always know. Ironically, they're usually the least qualified to show you the way. They've lived in their little universe, with their own language and activities. They have no capacity to interact with the great big world out there.

Stagnant waters stink.

God loves to show Himself to you in so many ways. I've heard His voice from a billboard, a song, complete silence, a pastor, a friend, and even someone I don't usually agree with.

We need a mixture of influences in our lives. As Proverbs 15:22 tells us, "Plans fail for lack of counsel, but with many advisers they succeed."

Looking Outward

CHAPTER 15

Don't Let Them Scare You

While in college, I chose to have people yell and scream at me in public. Why would I do this? Because I decided to be a basketball referee.

To make extra money and because I loved basketball, I refereed junior high and high school basketball games. Unfortunately, I quickly discovered I was in for loud opinions about my eyesight, occasional profanity, and heated comments about the rules and my judgment in almost every game.

You can never be a successful official if you let these kinds of criticism affect your decision-making in any way. You can't have "rabbit ears"—listening to every word thrown your way. If you did, you would never last long as a basketball official. But unfortunately, criticism comes with the territory.

Being a referee was going to serve me well later in life. It taught me how to handle myself in the public spotlight, deal with disagreements from passionate people, and persevere in the face of criticism until a job is complete.

Out of the hundreds of games I officiated, one high school game stands out above the rest. The game was in Muskogee, Oklahoma, between the Muskogee Roughers and the Tulsa East Central Cardinals. Muskogee was ranked number one in the state and had two future Division 1 college basketball players on its roster. East Central was an average team, and they had lost as many games as they'd won. It looked to be a one-sided game.

It was Muskogee's high school homecoming, and the entire arena was filled to capacity that Friday night. The Muskogee fans were happy, loud, and eager to celebrate a home-team win. But from the start, the visiting team from Tulsa was playing much better than expected. The score was tied at the end of the first quarter and again at halftime.

Muskogee was ahead by only one point early in the fourth quarter. Then one of their players drove to the basket and was clearly fouled by the tallest East Central player. I called the foul, and because it was the player's fifth foul, he had to leave the game.

As I was notifying the scorer's table who the foul was on and how many free throws the home team would be taking (two), I noticed that the East Central head coach had pulled all his players from the court and was talking to them in front of their bench.

This gathering of players was unusual, so I went over to the other official and asked him, "Did they call a time-out?"

"I didn't hear them call a time-out," he said.

So I walked over to the huddle in front of the bench, stuck my head in, and asked the head coach if he'd called a time-out. Instantly, he went crazy! Screaming, yelling, saying I didn't know the rules and other words I don't want to put in this book.

I immediately called a technical foul on him for that behavior. Then I had just turned to the scorer's table to notify them of the technical foul when suddenly, from behind, that coach grabbed my uniform at my shoulder and spun me around. As I was turning, in one fluid motion I assessed him his second technical foul and threw him out of the game.

The gym went bonkers! Muskogee fans were dancing, laughing, and screaming. Because of the personal foul and two technical fouls, the home team received six free throws and possession of the ball. They made five free throws, scored a basket on the inbound pass, and went on to win by twenty-four points.

The coach's outburst didn't make any sense at the time. No egregious comments had been made during the game by either coach, and the foul was evident to everyone. However, I later found out that the coach I sent home early got caught up in the game's emotion and mistakenly thought I didn't know what a coach can or cannot do when a player fouls out.

On the way home, I stopped and went into a convenience store to grab something to drink. The clerk looked at me, still in my black-and-white-striped uniform, and asked, "Who won?"

With a twinkle in my eye, I quickly replied, "I did."

When unmerited criticism comes, don't let it stop you, and you will win too!

Are you ever criticized? Criticism is a compliment when you're doing what's right. I've heard it said that false accusation is the last step before supernatural promotion. I've seen that be true many times. The best way to respond to those kind of people is to say, "If you stop telling lies about me, I'll stop telling the truth about you."

The first and greatest commandment about critics is *Don't let them scare you!* Never surrender your dream to noisy negatives. Author Greg King, among others, has been quoted as saying, "Do not argue with an idiot. He will drag you down to his level and beat you with experience."

Stop listening to the negative. Remember this thought: *not everyone has a right to speak into your life.* Nobody can make you feel average without your permission. Remember the saying "Other people's opinion of you is their truth, not yours. You don't have to be bound to it or burdened by it."

We're all being judged by somebody who isn't even close to having their act together.

You must understand that ingratitude and criticism will come; they're part of the price you pay to be uncommon. Many times others aren't necessarily against you as much as they're for themselves.

The fact is that when you make your mark in life, you will always attract erasers. So listen to the constructive and ignore the destructive. Counterpunch critics with your success and knock them out with a smile.

Have you ever noticed that those who don't succeed are always the first to tell you how to succeed? So don't accept criticism from those you would never go to for advice.

Several people have been credited with saying, "You'll never be criticized by someone doing more than you. You'll always be criticized by someone doing less." Remember that. You'll discover that people who dish out criticism predictably can't handle a drop of their own medicine.

For me to listen to your criticism, I must first value your opinion. Many would-be great moms, dads, spiritual leaders, and successful businesspeople aren't any of those successful people today because they couldn't stand the criticism and simply gave up. At Tiger Woods's induction into the World Golf Hall of Fame, he talked about not being allowed in clubhouses as a young, black, amateur golfer. Of that hostile atmosphere, he said, "I'd put my shoes on in the parking lot and ask two questions: Where's the first tee, and what's the course record?"

If Jesus, who was perfect in every way, was criticized, you will be too. Criticism will come from everywhere, even from those who love you. Like the wife who said, "My husband would take a bullet for me, but he would also criticize how I drove him to the hospital afterward."

Negative people need drama like oxygen. So stay positive, and it will take their breath away. Learn to use criticism as fuel, and you will never run out of energy. Never let someone else's words get in the way of your dreams.

Rapper Asher Roth notes, "Do your thing. Do it every day. Do it unapologetically. Don't be discouraged by criticism. You probably already know what they're going to say. Pay no mind to the fear of failure. It's far more valuable than success. Take ownership, take chances, and have fun. And no matter what, don't ever stop doing your thing."

Criticism is a compliment when you're doing what's right.

CHAPTER 16

Obstacle Course

In early 2020, I was out doing what I had done for more than thirty years—speaking. February took me to Daytona Beach, where I had the privilege of speaking to a large network marketing crowd. Later, the first weekend in March, I was in the pulpit of one of my favorite churches in America, Church on the Rock in St. Peters, Missouri.

I'd heard distant rumblings about a virus, and I remember being cautious and starting to think about keeping my distance from people. But life was about to change in an awful way. Astonishingly, only one week later, the Missouri church I had just preached in was no longer open to the public for services. The worldwide COVID-19 pandemic had begun.

Life was different for everyone. Never in my wildest dreams could I have imagined going up to a bank teller to ask for money while wearing a mask. But I did. There were also shortages of toilet paper. When I was growing up, there was so much toilet paper that people threw it up in the trees of their enemies. Yes, everything was changing. Can we all agree that in 2015 not a single person correctly answered the question, "Where do you see yourself five years from now?"

Every person on the face of the earth was about to have their life adversely affected by this demonic illness. Everything I was doing—and I mean everything—stopped, paused, or was canceled. And for the next couple of months, I had no new income or opportunities. I wondered what the future would be like. I found myself full of faith like never before yet frightened at the same time.

Thankfully, I knew that every obstacle introduces people to themselves and never leaves them the way it finds them. But I was about to live out these truths in a very real way.

I believed (and still do) that challenges create both problems *and* opportunities. But most importantly, I knew the Bible is true when it says, "We know that all things work together for good to those who love God, to those who are called according to His purpose" (Rom. 8:28 NKJV). I was determined to believe God's Word. I needed things to work for good in my life and my family's, and I sincerely believed that God would take care of us in every way. Part of my daily prayers was a request for provision and protection for every one of us.

The interesting fact about significant obstacles is that they create once-in-a-lifetime opportunities. This happened to me. Two of the most significant authors I've ever had the privilege of helping were about to come my way *only* because of the pandemic. Without this awful sickness, I would never have connected with either of them. Firsthand, I watched God's Word work.

One author was an international billionaire who told me he finally found himself in a position to write his long-desired autobiography only because of the pandemic. The second author is so famous I had to sign a three-page nondisclosure agreement to find out who he was and later a twelve-page writing contract. He told me he would never have had the time to create this book had it not been for the pandemic. The pandemic, of all things, had provided the opportunity for these gentlemen to write the books on their hearts.

Sometimes the bad things that happen in our lives put us directly on the path to the best things that will ever happen to us. God took something terrible and worked it for these men's good and mine. The experience of collaborating with them left me better than they found me. I grew in areas I'd never had the opportunity to grow in. God provided good in the middle of bad. That's what He does!

You can find this next story in several books.

One Sunday morning in a small Texas church, the new pastor called on one of the older deacons to lead the closing prayer. The deacon came up on the podium, stood by the pastor, bowed his head, and said, "Lord, I hate buttermilk!" The pastor opened one eye and wondered just where this was going.

The deacon continued, "Lord, I hate lard!" Now the pastor was totally perplexed.

The deacon continued, "And I ain't too crazy about plain flour neither, but after you mix 'em all together and bake 'em in a hot oven, I just love biscuits! So, Lord, help us understand that when life gets hard, when things come up that we don't like and we can't figure out what You're doing, we just need to wait and see what You're making. After You get through mixing and baking, it'll probably be something even better than biscuits. Amen!"

On the other side of the storm is a bright sunny day. When something bad happens, you have three choices: you can let it stop you, you can let it define you, or you can give it to God and trust Him to make something good out of it. Expect the positive even if you must believe a little longer. If you always see your glass as half-empty, just pour it into a smaller glass and stop complaining. Refuse to let a bad situation bring out the worst in you.

Choose joy. Not because everything is good but because you know God is good. Someone once said, "When storms come your way, remember you know the master of the wind. When sickness finds you, remember you know the Great Physician. When your heart gets broken, just say, 'I know the Potter.' It doesn't matter what we go through; Jesus is the way, the truth, and the life."

As I'm writing this book, the world isn't sure if the COVID pandemic is over or not. Or if it's an endemic now. But at one point during the pandemic, I began to wonder if I was getting a tan from the light in the refrigerator! My ministry friend Tim Walker said, "Whether this has been a great year, a horrible year, or a trail mix of both, there's something to celebrate. We tend to remember what we should forget and forget what we should remember. But the good news is you're still alive! You can either grieve over what you've lost or gather what you've got left, give it to God, and allow Him to do miracles with it!"

Regardless of what name people use to describe bad things, God will continue to take the bad and find the good for those who love Him and walk in His purpose. Amazing!

CHAPTER 17

Friends Become Our Chosen Family

I sensed the time was coming for me to end my time working in Florida. We'd moved there almost three years earlier to help turn around a struggling publishing company. God had done miraculous things there, and now the company was doing very well. Nevertheless, I believed it was time for a change, including our moving back to Tulsa. Linda and I didn't share this with anybody.

As we were considering our move, we went to an event to hear a speaker named Kathy, who was a minister and author I had helped publish two books. She was an admirable Bible teacher with a sense of humor and remarkable spiritual insight.

After her message, Kathy privately shared with Linda and me some things she felt in her heart from the Lord. She talked about a change that was coming and said Linda should show the Lord her heart's desire—designing it, ripping specific pictures of it out of magazines, and spreading it all out before Him. Linda was thrilled to hear this because it was a personal confirmation from the Lord that she should continue what she'd *already been doing*—tearing out pictures from magazines and compiling a folder full of what she specifically wanted in our next home.

Shortly thereafter, I attended a conference in Tulsa. It was important for me to be there to meet with some prominent ministers about their books. At the same time, I took advantage of the opportunity to look at houses in the area. I connected with an outstanding realtor who showed me seven homes, but none of them seemed to be a good fit for us.

I had finished looking at houses for the day when I reached out to my good friend and ministry board member, Tim Redmond. He invited me over for dinner, and I was looking forward to seeing him and his wife, Sandy.

As I was driving on the street that led to Tim's subdivision, I noticed a neighborhood to my right I'd never seen. Its entry gate had always been closed. But that evening it was open, and a small sign outside it said For Sale by Builder. I decided to pull into the neighborhood. It was one big circle with only a dozen or so beautiful homes. Each one sat on about an acre or more with majestic trees. Unfortunately, they also appeared to be very expensive.

Still, I decided to at least dream about living there and looked for the house for sale. As I drove around the circle, I saw a beautiful home with a gorgeous pool and waterfall in the backyard. I hesitated when I saw the For Sale by Builder sign was there, but I thought, *I have nothing to lose. I'll ring the doorbell and see if I can find out what the situation is.*

I parked my car in the semicircle driveway, stepped to the entrance, and rang the doorbell. A man answered the door, and before I could say anything, he said, "John Mason, what are you doing here? I thought you lived in Florida." I didn't know this man, but evidently he knew me. I told him I was considering moving back to Tulsa and was looking at houses while I was here. I admitted I'd been looking at homes no doubt in a lower price range than his.

He said, "Why don't you come in and look at my house anyway." Then he added, "Would you like to use my video recorder so you can show the house to your wife when you get back home? Furthermore, I have a special builder's mortgage that gives me a lot of flexibility in financing this house, and I might be able to make it available to a potential buyer."

Thinking I was out of my league but nevertheless interested, I walked throughout the beautiful house and made the recording. I knew Linda was still creating a dream-house folder based on what Kathy had encouraged her to do, and I generally knew the highlights. I started thinking, *A lot of this is what Linda wants, and it would be a perfect fit for our four kids.* As I finished my walk-through, the builder shared the price and the special financing, which made buying the house a possibility. Feeling more hopeful, I left and drove less than a half mile away to my friend Tim's home.

As we ate dinner together, Tim and Sandy were fascinated to hear about what houses I'd seen. I described some of them but explained that none of them seemed to be a fit. Then I said, "And there's one I'm not sure I can afford, but it's a beautiful home with everything we need and more, right down the street from you."

I could see Tim's eyes getting bigger and bigger as I described the house. When I'd finished, he said excitedly, "I know that house. It's a great house. I was actually there several times while

76

it was being built. As I looked at it, I really felt in my heart that I should get out of my car, walk around the home, and say this prayer over it: 'I call this house into the ministry. I call this house into the ministry.'"

Here's my ministry board member telling me he had prayed "this house into the ministry" months earlier! It was evident to me that God was very much up to something here for my family. I also explained the financing arrangement to Tim. He was knowledgeable about that type of loan and was completely positive about our possibly using that approach to buy what would be a miraculous house for us.

When I returned home, I told Linda I had something exciting to show her and played the video I'd made of the house. It showed everything she'd drawn, torn out, and placed in her folder, plus additional helpful and beautiful features that weren't in there. Doesn't that sound like God? The house was precisely what Linda had prayed for.

Of course, we bought that house, then moved back to Tulsa and lived in it with our four kids for almost twenty years. It was a blessing. God knew what we needed. He used people to show us and confirm what we should do. "There will always be a reason why you meet certain people. Either you need them to change your life or you're the one who will change theirs," said Angel Flonis Harefa.

Thank you, Kathy, for speaking that word to Linda, and thank you, Tim, for praying over that house and encouraging me. God blesses His people through people, and that's why associations are so critical. Who you associate with incredibly affects your life for the good or the bad.

A sure way God helps us be uncommon is through friends. I genuinely believe God cares a lot about who we choose as friends. Proverbs 13:20 tells us, "He who walks with wise men will be wise, but the companion of fools will be destroyed" (NKJV). I look for friends who walk in wisdom. You become like those you associate with. Proverbs 27:19 says, "A mirror reflects a man's face, but what he is really like is shown by the kind of friends he chooses" (TLB). If you associate with four uncommon friends, you'll be uncommon. But if you associate with four common friends, you'll be common.

Good friends will bring the good out in you. They accept you as you are and are part of helping you become who you should be. These friends leave you better than they found you. They light up your life. So "stay close to those who feel like sunshine," as someone once quipped.

As you grow in the Lord, who some of your friends are will change. You will need new friends. You'll need to say no to some friends and spend less time with others. That's not always easy to do, but you must. Say goodbye, but treasure the good memories you created together.

I try to stay away from "still" people. Still angry. Still stuck. Still making excuses. Still telling the same story. Still stuck in the past. Still not working. Still words, not deeds. Still broke. Still using the same alibi. Still thinking about revenge. Still no action. Still offended. Still blaming God.

I want "are" people in my life. Are godly. Are dependable. Are of good report. Are integrous. Are faithful. Are helpful. Are hardworking. Are enthusiastic. Are loyal. Are kind. Are uncommon. Are trustworthy. Are cheerful. Are brave. Are walking in God's will.

You can tell who your best friends are—they accept your imperfections, help you grow in God, make you laugh until you cry, and cause you to smile every time you see them. They help you up when no one else knows you've stumbled. They make happy times better and difficult times easier.

As someone said, "Great friends know how crazy you are and still choose to be seen with you in public. Together, you and your best friends will probably be causing trouble in nursing homes someday."

CHAPTER 18

Keep Going—It's the Only Way to Get Where You're Supposed to Be

It's 1943, and World War II is raging.

A young boy stands on a downtown Jackson, Mississippi, street corner early every morning and late into the evening selling newspapers. At the same time, he's selling war stamps to support the war effort.

Born in a charity hospital, he was raised in the poorest part of town, and most of his young friends are now in jail. He has no brothers, no sisters, no aunts, no uncles. After the boy's father passed away when he was ten, he became the sole provider for his illiterate mother and himself.

There's a contest across America to see who can sell the most war stamps. In the most unlikely of success stories, this boy has sold twelve million dollars' worth of them. The second-place finisher? Four million dollars. As a result, he wins a trip to meet the president of the United States, and with a borrowed suit two sizes too big, he heads to Washington, DC, for the journey of a lifetime.

Later, this young man serves his community as a firefighter for nine years, one day rescuing a young girl no one else can save. He graduates from Hinds Junior College in Mississippi, then marries a pretty brunette from Indiana, and soon after graduates from the Indiana University School of Business.

After serving his country in the army, he runs a successful branch office for his employer, earning more than thirty consecutive years of profit. All the while, he never loses the balance of loving his wife, loving his kids, and loving his God.

A real success in my eyes. Ultimate success.

He was the best man at my wedding. He was easily the hardest-working man I've ever worked with. And when you consider where he started, the obstacles he overcame, and how he ended up, he was the most successful man I knew.

I think of him today as I write this book. You see, that boy was my dad, Chester Mason. Against all the odds and despite all the obstacles, he made it.

My dad never made a big deal about what he had to overcome. He just did it because he didn't want to stay where he was. He wanted a better life for himself and his family.

Sometimes, when I doubt how far I can go, I just remember how far my dad came in life. I saw everything he faced, all the battles he won, and all the fears he overcame. All the best stories have one thing in common: you must go against the odds to reach your dreams.

When you focus on your difficulties, you'll have more difficulties. When you focus on opportunities, you'll have more opportunities. When someone tells you, "It can't be done," it's more a reflection of their limited thinking, not yours.

Overcoming obstacles impacts your life and all those connected to you now and in the future. So if you're unsure about pressing on, remember that others depend on you. One day you'll tell your story of how you overcame what you're going through now, and it will become part of someone else's inspiration to keep moving forward.

The secret to ultimate success is to take what you have and move forward by faith no matter what obstacles you face. You didn't come this far to come only this far.

No obstacle leaves you the way it found you. Either you will be better or you will be worse. God knows obstacles along your journey are there to prepare you for the blessings that await you at the finish line.

When I consider my dad's life, I agree with Booker T. Washington, who said, "I have learned that success is to be measured not so much by the position that one has reached in life as by the obstacles which he has overcome while trying to succeed."

CHAPTER 19

God Blesses People through People

While working as an executive at a publishing company, I began to desire writing a book myself. I had never even remotely considered writing one until then. I mainly received Bs in English, while it was to my wife, not to me, that teachers said, "We're going to read books from you someday!"

Yet I strongly felt I should write a book. So I did the only thing I knew to do: I bought a book on how to write a book. Not just any book. *The* book, *The Elements of Style*. But after reading it, I was entirely convinced I could never do it.

God had another plan.

I decided to have lunch with a married couple I respected from the publishing company. She was over the editorial department, and he was the top information technology person. We met at a favorite Mexican restaurant.

Over chips and salsa, I jumped into the conversation by telling them how I felt I should write a book, but it looked impossible to me. Immediately, they both said I should do it!

If you find yourself in a ditch, others can't help you unless you let them know you're stranded. Be wise enough to know when you need help and have the boldness to let go and ask for it. Be courageous. Ask someone to help you. You don't have to go it alone. You weren't made to be a one-person show. A key to being successful is to admit when you don't know something and ask for help.

I still remember the excitement in their voices. They'd been in many devotional settings where I'd spoken, and they told me, "You need to be yourself. You like to tell stories; share short, pithy sayings; and encourage everyone. You also don't waste people's time when you speak. Your words are memorable."

Suddenly, I could see how I could do it. Be me. Be clear. Be short. Be funny. Be encouraging.

Be myself!

I started writing, taking small steps, determined to stay true to myself. And in a little over two years, my first book was completed.

Then God lined up a second person to again change my limited thinking. I'll never forget the day the book arrived at the office. There it was, all shiny and new, with a decent picture of me on the cover. (A good photograph is one that doesn't really look like you. Have you noticed people rarely look like their picture? I've been guilty of this, having left my late-thirty-something picture on my book cover for nearly twenty years. So I guess we'll leave the photo because it looks good. And looks even better as the years progress.)

I took my book into Pat Judd's office. Pat is a good friend, and he was about to rock my little world with his words.

I told him I had "high expectations" for the book. Even though I knew the average book released by established publishers sold only around five thousand copies at that time, I was hoping my self-published book would sell the same—maybe even ten thousand!

Pat looked at me and sincerely said, "If this doesn't sell one hundred thousand copies, I'll be disappointed."

My friend was a top executive in book sales and marketing, so he knew what he was talking about. But something happened when he spoke those words about my book: a lid flew off! My expectations dramatically changed. Now the sky was the limit, meaning the book and I had no limits at all. I had known my limits, and now I was ignoring them! I was determined to set goals that scared me and excited me at the same time.

The rest is history. As I mentioned in an earlier chapter, *An Enemy Called Average* has sold more than seven hundred thousand copies, and it's been published in numerous languages worldwide.

I've seen that when God gets ready to bless you, He often sends a person (or maybe a married couple) into your life. No one is sent to anyone by accident. God uses people to help people.

Spending time with God and those He connects you with puts everything else in the proper perspective.

Words matter. Especially those from the people God sends your way.

What we see depends mainly on what we look for and who we listen to. What I saw was a book I couldn't write, but if I did, one that would moderately sell. God sent people to me to change my perspective and my hope. Something changed. Immediately. Now I could write the book. God set it up for me to talk with individuals who made me see the world and my future differently.

Please believe me when I say the Bible is true when it says,

> Now to Him who is able to [carry out His purpose and] do superabundantly more than all that we dare ask or think [infinitely beyond our greatest prayers, hopes, or dreams], according to His power that is at work within us, to Him be the glory in the church and in Christ Jesus throughout all generations forever and ever. Amen. (Eph. 3:20–21 AMP)

Don't downgrade your dream just to fit your reality. Instead, upgrade your belief to match your destiny.

I believe God sends people into our lives to speak "a word in season" for us. It's undoubtedly one of the ways He talks to us—through others. It's almost impossible for me to believe you'd have this book to read without those people God sent at the right time, at the right place, to speak into my life. He will send people to you too. Be open to them.

CHAPTER 20

People Matter to God

I was excited and nervous. I'd been invited to speak at a large church for their Sunday night service. Several thousand people would be there, and I already knew what I felt I should share.

I was honored to be invited and looked forward to that evening's service. I was already in town, so I attended the Sunday morning service, which went ahead as usual—singing, announcements, and offering. Then before the sermon began, the pastor announced that this was "missionary Sunday," so they would be taking up a second offering for their missionaries. *OK*, I thought, *that's good*. I made a second donation.

As that collection ended, a man walked up front and described a special need within the church. It was a worthy cause, a much-needed area of ministry. As he finished, we were told there would be a special offering for that need too. The buckets were passed for the third time. I don't remember if I gave. I do remember feeling a little uneasy.

When Sunday night arrived, I was ready. The service began, and it was a wonderful time of worship and singing. Then it was offering time.

Yes, what happened in the morning service was repeated in the evening service. Three more offerings! I knew most people there had been present that morning, which meant they were asked to give six times that day!

I gave my message, and it was well received. Thank God.

As I was returning to my seat, the congregation was informed that a special offering would be taken up *for me.* One, two, three, four, five, six, seven times these dear people were asked to give this day! I was embarrassed. I wanted to say, "Forget it," but I didn't. The buckets were already being passed—again.

I'm not saying what happened was *wrong*; the church did have worthy causes. But it certainly wasn't *right.* I'm thankful for opportunities to give to God's work, but sometimes too much of a good thing is way too much.

People are not a means to an end. People are the end. Every one of them matters to God. Mother Teresa reminded us that each person we serve is "Jesus in disguise."

You and I might not ask for seven offerings from those with whom we work and live every day, but I think we can all treat others better. So everywhere we go, let's look at others not as a means but as the end.

Author Eric Hoffer notes, "Rudeness is the weak man's imitation of strength." Never take advantage of someone. We all reap what we sow. Sow mercy, and you'll receive mercy. Sow generosity, and people will be generous back to you. Sow a smile, and watch how you light up another person's life!

Be kind when possible—and it's always possible.

See people as God sees them, and don't judge them by what they wear, the color of their skin, where they live, what they drive, the job they have, or how they speak. It's God's idea to care for people regardless of what they can give back to us. Everyone deserves respect and kindness.

If you genuinely love others, you'll want what's best for them, whether or not that includes you. And how you make others feel about themselves says a lot about you. As writer and orator Robert Ingersoll said, "We rise by lifting others."

If you can be one thing, be kind. What means most in life is what you've done for others. Most people can smile for two months on five words of praise and a pat on the back. Kindness doesn't cost a dime. Sprinkle it everywhere.

Build others up. Put their insecurities to rest. Remind them they're worthy. Tell them they're incredible. Be a light in their darkness.

Put others first. No one is more deceived or cheated than a selfish person. You and I were created to help others.

I love it when I have the opportunity to speak, whether in a church or business setting. I almost always say to myself afterward, *This is why I was created, and I want to do this more.* I think the basis for this feeling is that, long ago, I realized I was there for the audience; the audience wasn't there for me.

As I prepare to speak somewhere—and when I'm there—I'm careful to remind myself that I'm there to serve others. So my usual prayer is this: "Lord, I'm the lowest in the room; I'm here as a servant. So use me however You want to bless and encourage Your people."

Dr. Tony Evans once said, "When you realize God's purpose for your life isn't just about you, He will use you in a mighty way."

There are two types of people in the world: those who come into a room and say, "Here I am!" and those who come into a room and say, "Ah, *there* you are!" So how do you know a good person? A good person makes others feel good. Find happiness by helping others find it.

Satisfaction means we go to sleep at night knowing our talents and gifts were used in a way that served others. So no matter how educated, talented, rich, or fabulous you believe you are, how you treat people ultimately tells all.

Never think that what you have to offer is worthless. There will always be someone who needs what you have. "You'll never be happy if you chase money and stuff all of your life, but you can find true joy through giving and serving others," finance expert Dave Ramsey reminds us.

I've heard it said, "There comes a point in your life when you realize who matters, who never did, who won't anymore, and who always will. And in the end, you learn who is fake, who is true, and who would risk it all for you."

Be *that* person, the one who puts others before yourself.

CHAPTER 21

Invest in Others—
the Return Can Be Eternal

Unfortunately, I found myself on a church board trying to deal with the moral failure of its leader. As the former pastor and his wife began to navigate the restoration and rebuilding of their marriage, I had a conversation with him about where he found himself.

"I am fully responsible for my actions," he quietly said. "I'm going back to the basics, back to my first love in my relationship with God."

As we continued to talk, he added, "What's revealing to me is how many people are completely gone from our lives now. We have hardly any relationships left—even with the six fellow pastors responsible for my restoration. Not one has contacted me." I remember looking at him and saying, "Jim [not his real name], you're not worth the risk to them."

Jesus hung out with people like Jim. He took risks with tax collectors, prostitutes, and gentiles. I believe that's where He most wanted to be. It's the sick who need a physician, as He said (Luke 5:31). But don't we *all* need the loving, healing touch of the Great Physician?

God sends people into our lives we're supposed to take risks on—people others run from or ignore. But unfortunately, doing this for others is rare.

Sherman (not his real name), who lived alone with his mother in a run-down old farmhouse, was someone no one had anything to do with in high school. He was an awkward young man, intellectually slow and always disheveled. His hair was never combed and was littered with dandruff. And he always smelled—in a way you remembered.

Sherm and I became friends. I don't know why I gravitated toward him; I stayed away from plenty of other odd kids in school. But Sherm was someone I wanted to be friends with. I knew he needed a friend.

Some days I would pick him up for school and take him home afterward. I'd buy him pizza and take him to school events. And one time I managed to arrange a double date for him and me. I talked to him about the Lord and knew he had a personal relationship with God.

Sherm was always quiet, I guess in the kind of way outcasts can be. He wanted to be liked, just as all of us do, especially in high school. I knew my friendship meant a lot to him. But what he did for me touched me more than anything I ever did for him.

I saw how blessed I was and how everyone—*everyone*—matters to God. I felt assigned to Sherm, and in a divine way, he was assigned to me during our high school years.

I lost track of Sherm when I moved eight hundred miles away to attend college. I heard he got a job and was working the best he could. I've never forgotten his impact on my life perspective.

I believe God sends people across our path not just to be a blessing to us but, more importantly, so we can be a blessing to them. You don't need a reason to help others.

I challenge you to pray this life-changing, dangerous (in a good way) prayer: "Lord, send those into my life I can bless. Show me how to love them as You love them. And may they come to know You because I loved them too."

A good deed bears interest. I believe that one of the marks of lasting greatness is to develop greatness in others.

I have found that outstanding people have a unique perspective—that greatness is deposited into them not to stay but rather to flow through them into others.

Whatever we praise, we increase. So share some hope and encouragement with others.

Your opportunity may not look or act like Sherm. But I know every one of us has people in our lives we can help. No investment you can make will pay you so well as investing in the improvement of others throughout your life.

CHAPTER 22

Learn from Others— You Can't Make Enough Mistakes on Your Own

Let me tell you two stories—one true, the other legendary. Until it was torn down in 2007, Zingo was a famous local roller coaster where we live here in Tulsa. It featured nearly a ninety-foot drop and a fifty-mile-per-hour speed. It was built by hand in 1968 and constructed out of wood and steel. The wood framing made it feel and sound a little rickety, which added to the frightfulness of the ride.

It was a good, fast roller coaster.

My daughter, Michelle, was eight years old, and for months she'd been asking me to take her on the Zingo now that she was just tall enough to ride it. I wasn't sure how it would go, but I said yes, and off we went to Bell's Amusement Park, where the Zingo awaited us.

Excited, we stood in line waiting our turn, watching each group of nearly all young people ride the coaster. Some screamed, others closed their eyes, but most were having a great time.

Finally, it was our turn. We got into our seat, the very front one. The attendant "locked" us in by lowering a bar in front of us, but there was so much space between Michelle and the bar that she couldn't reach it. And there was an opening to her right, where we had entered our seat. I saw her initial fright, so I put my arm around her.

Off we slowly went up the first climb. I had ridden the Zingo before and knew the first drop was the biggest, so I looked at Michelle to see how she was doing. Her eyes were fixed ahead, her arms wrapped around me in a death grip. To add to the anticipation, the ride's designers had added a *click, click, click* to each foot or two as we slowly moved skyward.

About three-quarters of the way up, Michelle's fear transformed into a full scream—and we weren't even at the top yet. In a few seconds, we would drop nearly ninety feet at fifty miles per hour!

Thinking she was about to be flung from her seat, a certain death, she held on to me even tighter and screamed louder. She continued screaming from the first drop until the moment the coaster finally ground to a halt, back where we started. Alive, but in my case with diminished hearing in the ear closest to my daughter (not really).

This is a memory Michelle and I will never forget.

Here's the second story, often told to make a point.

An elderly Florida lady did her shopping, and upon returning to the parking lot, she found four males in the act of leaving with her vehicle. She dropped her shopping bags and drew her handgun, screaming at the top of her lungs, "I have a gun, and I know how to use it! Get out of the car!"

The four men didn't wait for a second invitation; they got out of the car and ran like mad. The lady, somewhat shaken, then proceeded to load her shopping bags into the back of the car and get into the driver's seat. She was so shaken that she couldn't get her key into the ignition. She tried and tried, and then it dawned on her why she was having trouble.

A few minutes later, she found her own car parked four or five spaces farther down. She loaded her bags into the car and drove straight to the police station. The sergeant to whom she told the story nearly tore himself in two with laughter. He pointed to the other end of the counter, where four pale men were reporting a carjacking by a mad, elderly woman described as white and less than five feet tall, with glasses, curly white hair, and carrying a large handgun.

No charges were filed.

The moral of these two stories?

Sometimes in life, we're the little old lady. We're sure we're right and make everyone react to what we "know" to be true. But maybe we're wrong. That creates havoc, and we need to make it right.

Sometimes we're the four men. Minding our own business, suddenly surprised to find ourselves ousted from our comfort zone for no apparent reason, only to discover that we were right all along. And then we're able to go back to what we were doing before, only now with a new perspective and appreciation along with a smile on our faces.

Sometimes we're the ambitious person wanting to ride a "Zingo." We've all been told the best way to overcome our fears is to confront them. And that is true. It's also true that when you get to do something you've always wanted to do, you may be disappointed or even scared once you're there. In any case, you'll discover something about yourself you didn't know before.

It's never too late to do better. God expands our horizons every time we turn to Him. The more we get to know God, the more we discover how much more there is to know about Him. He wants to fill every void and every opportunity in our lives.

Life is like a roller coaster. We can either scream every time there's a bump or throw our hands up in the air and enjoy the ride. Our heavenly Father is with us through all the twists and turns, ups and downs, from the beginning to the end.

CHAPTER 23

Success Is a Series of Small Wins

Have you ever felt belittled when asked questions like "Are you in *full-time* ministry? Are you traveling to *many* nations? Are you winning *thousands* to the Lord?"

Don't fall into the trap that says you matter to God only if you're doing or saying *big* things. Mother Teresa said, "Not all of us can do great things. But we can do small things with great love."

God is in the little things. Everything is important when you're doing His will. Don't fall into the comparison trap, the trap that says what you're doing is too small, too unimportant compared to what others are doing. Stop trying to be like everybody—you don't even *like* everybody.

"The way we do small things determines the way we do every-thing," notes writer Robin Sharma.[1]

Allow yourself small victories. Don't deny giving yourself credit for accomplishing something, no matter how insignificant it might seem at the time. Instead of doing nothing today because you're overwhelmed or full of fear, do something even if it's small—because then you'll be one step closer to your goal.

Small goes where big can't.

Years ago, I was in a hurry to get to where I was going, and after turning off my car's engine, I dropped my keys into the abyss between the driver's seat and the center console. Every driver knows that place—dark, narrow, and hard to navigate. Fortunately for me, my six-year-old son, Mike, was with me. When I asked him if he could get Dad's keys, he willingly stuck his little hand into the spot and quickly retrieved them.

His small hand could go where my big hand couldn't. (Incidentally, Mike became so good at finding things that even now, when he's an adult, our family frequently turns to him—or to the grandkids!—when we can't find something.)

Don't underestimate or despise where you are and what you're doing right now. God starts where you are—always. It's how He takes you from where you are to where He wants you to be.

Everything big starts with something small.

Success is found in small things done well every day, so do one small thing to make today better than yesterday. Here's a prayer I like to pray for myself and suggest for other people: "Lord, send small opportunities into my life so I can use what You've put inside me to help others."

In the film *The Hobbit*, based on the book by J. R. R. Tolkien, the character Gandalf says, "Saruman believes it is only great power that can hold evil in check, but that is not what I have found. It is the small everyday deeds of ordinary folk that keep the darkness at bay. Small acts of kindness and love."[2]

If you can't help a hundred people, then help just one. When children fall fifty times as they learn to walk, they never think, *Maybe this isn't for me*. No, they keep on taking those small steps, and before long, they're running. This idea puts a humorous frame on it: "If you think you are too small to be effective, you have never been in the dark with a mosquito."

I fell in love with my wife because of the hundreds of tiny things she never knew she was doing that made me smile. The best times of your life will be the small, seemingly insignificant moments you spend smiling and laughing with someone who matters to you. Love is a big thing built of little things.

What looks like a small act to you may be a very big thing to another person. Small daily improvements are the key to staggering, long-term results.

CHAPTER 24

Don't Add to Your Life Those Who Subtract from Your Life

About a year and a half after my first book came out, my life and ministry were exploding. God was opening amazing doors for me to speak, and the book was selling thousands of copies every month. I was in a season of great harvest.

I thought this would be the perfect time to visit a well-known and respected Christian leader I'd known since college for counsel about navigating what the future might hold for me. The appointment was set, and I was looking forward to it and had my questions all lined up.

I was about to learn some valuable lessons.

Our thirty-minute meeting began with my sharing all the incredible things God was doing in my life—great responses when I spoke and prayed for people, substantial book sales all over the world, and more. I ended my description by saying, "You have a solid and respected ministry, and you know me. So I thought now would be a perfect time to come to you. I'm here to open up my life to your wisdom. I want you to speak into my life."

His words were not at all what I expected. The only way I know how to describe what happened is that he started talking to me like I was a first-year Bible school student he didn't know.

"Well, don't buy a computer—I've seen too many ministers waste too much of their money there."

Then, "Don't think that what's happening in your ministry now will continue to happen as it is."

And, "Do everything through your local church, and make sure you hire an ugly secretary."

All with a few more general, canned thoughts.

It was like I wasn't there. I don't know if he was just being careful or simply incapable of imparting wisdom into a person doing so much outside his church. I certainly felt he didn't want to take any risks in his "recommendations" to me.

Although I didn't get much out of the meeting itself, I took away several valuable lessons I've used from that day forward. Let me share some of them with you.

When a person can no longer contribute to your life, it's time to stop going to them for direction. Sometimes your circle as a whole decreases in size but increases in value.

Don't let it throw you if someone you respect and expect affirmation from doesn't or isn't able to give it to you.

Just because someone has known you for a long time doesn't mean they have anything to contribute to your future. Some people have no ability to see outside their world into yours. They're simply unable to relate to or care about anyone outside their world. They're an authority on only one subject—themselves and what *they* do. Maybe you can learn from them regarding administrative details, but they can't speak into *your* life, into *your* world. So why let them?

My main point is if somebody has nothing to contribute, why talk, listen, or receive from them? As we begin to grow outside their box, they become much more irrelevant as guides. Although their advice may be well-intended, they may intentionally give you nebulous, impersonal advice to decrease their risk if something goes wrong and makes them look bad.

Surrounding yourself with low-thinking people can limit your dreams to doing the same thing repeatedly and with the same crowd. It creates a limited life, because when you let other people define your world, they always make it too small. God knows who should be in your life and who shouldn't. Trust Him and let go. Whoever He knows should be there will still be there.

The quality of your thinking impacts the quality of your life. Attract people with creative minds and contagious commitment to their dreams. People will either stretch your vision or shrink your dream.

You are destined for so much more!

CHAPTER 25

Today Is the Opportunity You've Been Praying For

I t was a beautiful Thursday, and I'd taken the afternoon off and was out playing golf with my son Greg. As usual, he was beating me.

My cell phone rang, and I answered. It was a long-distance call. The founder of Get Motivated Seminars, Peter Lowe, was calling from his plane as he flew over the Atlantic Ocean from London to the States.

"John, I want you to speak for me next Tuesday at our event in North Carolina, taking Larry King's place on the platform." I'd heard that Larry King had just received emergency heart surgery. Now I was to be his substitute!

I told Peter, "Of course I will; I'd be honored." I hung up, then played lousy the rest of the round. This was the "big time." I would be speaking along with Barbara Bush, Dick Vitale, Zig

Ziglar, and several other famous speakers. Peter told me I would be closing the event (as Larry King usually did), so I needed to "knock it out of the park" and leave people feeling great.

I arrived the day before the event because I wanted to make sure I was prepared and ready to go, but I didn't sleep very well. I had the same vivid dream over and over. I was standing behind the stage, hearing an announcement that said Larry King would not be here tonight, so instead, we'd have . . . John Mason!

As I dreamed, I saw thirteen thousand people streaming out of the arena as I tried to give the best speech of my life to a moving target.

Of course, nothing like that happened. Peter did a great job introducing me, the speech went well, and the crowd was great. I got to meet a lot of famous people backstage. An hour with Dick Vitale talking basketball was unforgettable. Plus, now I get to tell you this story.

Remember, what you fear rarely happens. You lose when you let fear keep you from doing what you're afraid to do. Although I could have viewed this invitation and its timing as too intimidating to accept, I didn't. I kept in mind that it was a great opportunity, and I knew God wanted me to do it.

Excuses will always be there for you. Opportunities won't. CEO of Dell Technologies Michael Dell notes, "Don't spend so much time trying to choose the perfect opportunity that you miss the right opportunity." The truth is we don't get unlimited opportunities. And nothing is more disappointing than missing a life-changing opportunity.

Our walk with God begins with the word *follow* and ends with the word *go!* The devil hates hearing a believer say, "I'll do what You tell me to do, Lord." Go ahead. You never know what good will be on the other side of your action. God sends the opportunity, but it's up to us to act.

Opportunities are impatient and may not wait for you, so try to be ready for the opportunity before the opportunity is there. Opportunity dances with those already on the dance floor.

Availability is the most significant ability you can have. There's always time and opportunity. When opportunity knocks at your front door, don't be lost looking for four-leaf clovers in the backyard.

Seize the moment. Be ready. Say yes! Some opportunities don't knock twice. Your turn is here. It's time to *be uncommon*.

CHAPTER 26

I Forgive You—Goodbye

Have you ever been ripped off or taken advantage of? Shortly after graduating from college, I met a man I'll call Ron who seemed to be working with several influential people in Christian leadership around the country. I didn't know it yet, but he was also gaining a reputation in the Christian business community as a "big talker."

He wanted to meet with me, and I agreed. He talked about the consulting work he was doing with churches and ministries, and he asked if I wanted to help him accomplish some of the work.

I left our meeting excited because I had wanted to help people in leadership. We began to do some work together, but almost from the beginning, there was a problem: he wasn't paying me. Of course, he promised to pay me. There just always seemed to be some reason he couldn't. Yet I knew *he* was getting paid for the work *we* did.

I also noticed some patterns in his life: He exaggerated every-thing. He intentionally arrived late to meetings to make others wait on him as a power move and then bragged about it to me. He talked about anticipated projects as a way to keep me reserving time for them in my schedule, but the more I waited, the more he owed me for that time. I felt trapped.

Don't trust words, and question actions, but never doubt patterns.

Of course, Linda didn't trust this guy from the very start. She discerned something wasn't right. I was young and dumb and at the time didn't understand the incredible insight women can have. In fact, I rather stupidly said I was the one with the business degree in response to some of her strong hesitancies.

Our finances were getting very tight, but I felt I couldn't leave because this man owed me so much money and kept saying it was coming any day. But my stubbornness caused a financial hole in which I found myself going deeper and deeper.

Finally, I knew I should have nothing to do with Ron and that walking away would be the best thing I could do. I set up a meeting with him for 8:00 a.m. I knew he wouldn't be there on time, so at 8:01, I left. About thirty minutes later, I got an angry phone call from him demanding to know where I was. I told him I was gone, and I wasn't coming back.

Don't be where you're not supposed to be. We all must know what bridges to cross and which ones to burn. Remember the saying "Don't blame a clown for acting like a clown. Ask your-self why you keep going to the circus."

I later learned this man never intended to pay me and planned to use me for free as long as he possibly could. As a result, I found myself in a challenging financial situation that took a long time to rectify. All because of his lies. I was furious at him for what he'd done to my family and me.

Several years later, God was blessing our lives and ministry when I heard Ron was in a problematic situation. I must admit, I was glad he was in trouble. Over the years after I disconnected from him, I'd heard of other people he'd ripped off, and I felt like he was getting what he deserved.

Then one day I clearly felt the Lord speak to my heart, telling me to reach out to Ron, pray for him, and encourage him. Of course, at that point I would much rather have encouraged any other person on the face of the earth. But I knew beyond a shadow of a doubt that the Lord was directing me to do it. I don't know if theologically it's fair to say the Lord was testing me to see how sincere I was about being in the ministry and being an encourager, but I did sense there was more in this for me than for Ron. I believe God was watching to see if I would obey.

I picked up the phone and called him. He was surprised to hear from me. Before he could say something that might make me angry again, I took control of the conversation. "Ron, you still owe me a lot of money, and you weren't honest with me. But I forgive you for everything you told me that wasn't true." I then proceeded to encourage him with my words and from God's Word in every way I possibly could—and I even prayed for him.

By forgiving Ron, I discovered that forgiveness is the antidote for the poison of revenge. Forgiveness begins when your offense turns to prayer.

I can't say it felt fantastic doing this. It did, however, feel right. Forgiveness has that power. I felt lighter. I stopped thinking about Ron. I sincerely didn't care about what he'd done to me anymore. Finally, I closed the book on it. That chapter was over.

Forgiveness is about choosing to be free to focus on what God has ahead for us. Brigitte Nicole says, "One of the most courageous decisions you'll ever make is to finally let go of what is hurting your heart and soul."

Forgiveness is more powerful than we realize. It causes us to live in the present even though the past hurts. An unknown author once said, "I never knew how strong I was until I had to forgive someone who wasn't sorry and accepted an apology I never received."

Sometimes the first step to forgiveness is understanding the other person is a complete idiot—and maybe you were too. People make mistakes, so don't let one mistake ruin a good relationship. When someone does something wrong, don't forget all the things they did right.

Dr. Steve Maraboli advises, "The truth is, unless you let go, unless you forgive yourself, unless you forgive the situation, unless you realize that the situation is over, you cannot move forward." Keep your face forward by walking in forgiveness. Stop continually looking at your bruises. Live in the sunshine of forgiveness.

Ephesians 4:32 says, "Be kind and compassionate to one another, forgiving each other, just as in Christ God forgave you." And Matthew 6:14 tells us, "If you forgive other people when they sin against you, your heavenly Father will also forgive you." I need God's forgiveness. How about you?

Situations can change quickly, so if given the opportunity to forgive, do it. You don't know when you may have that opportunity again. Forgive everyone, including yourself, and go to sleep at night with a clean heart. When you forgive, you turn the person and the situation over to God and let Him work.

In his book *God's Power to Change Your Life*, Pastor Rick Warren writes, "To begin loving people today, we must close the door on the past. And that cannot happen without forgiveness! Forgive those who have hurt you—for your sake, not because they deserve it."[1]

Forgive others as often and as much as you'd like God to forgive you.

CHAPTER 27

Don't Get Boxed In

Early in my career, I was a consultant to a new church and their fledgling Christian school. As is usually the case with private Christian schools, they had an honor and dress code that students and staff were expected to sign and adhere to. I soon discovered that the entire code was built around how the pastor looked, dressed, talked, and believed. Imagine a forty-plus-year-old person as the ideal standard for kids ages five through eighteen.

It didn't take me long to learn that the more you were like this leader, the more you were celebrated. The less you were like him, the more you were criticized. People there found themselves using his phrases instead of their own to express themselves.

Of course, those who don't fit into a box like this are always labeled rebellious and disobedient. Jesus focuses on the *why*, but controllers always focus on the *what*. Some people will like you only if you fit inside their box. So don't be afraid to ship that box off to Timbuktu!

When you work with people who have found that what they believe is the perfect Christian model, you'll soon find out they never know what to do with individuals who don't fit into that model. Furthermore, if they don't fit, there must be something wrong with them.

Keep your distance from people who will never admit that they made a mistake and who always try to make you feel like *you* did something wrong. Never let anyone make you feel like you're less of a person. They have the problem, not you.

No single, suitable Christian model exists other than Jesus. Romans 12:2 says, "Don't copy the behavior and customs of this world, but be a new and different person with a fresh newness in all you do and think. Then you will learn from your own experience how his ways will really satisfy you" (TLB). We aren't called to be like other Christians; we're called to be like Christ.

God creates completely unique individuals, whereas too many leaders invent a single mold to which all must conform. And it usually looks, talks, and acts like them. It's laughable.

People may dislike you for being yourself, but deep inside, they wish they had the courage to do the same. The reward for being like everyone else is that everyone will like you—except you.

"Be daring, be different, be impractical, be anything that will assert integrity of purpose and imaginative vision against the play-it-safers, the creatures of the commonplace, the slaves of the ordinary," Sir Cecil Beaton declared.

God loves variety! More than twenty thousand known species of ferns grow around the world, and they're universally recognized as one of the hardiest plants. It doesn't make sense to me that God made that many different kinds of ferns, but this shows us how much He loves diversity. Think this: *I will never apologize for being me. Others should apologize for asking me to be anything else.*

In a controlling environment, conformity is celebrated. As a result, you can fall into the trap of judging how you're doing spiritually by how much you act, sound, and look like the leader. Imagine if everyone in the body of Christ looked like a foot, or an ear, or an arm. You don't have to know all the answers, and you don't have to find or follow someone who says they do.

People say, "Be yourself." But when you are, they say, "Not like that." So don't waste time trying to be someone else. Everybody likes conformity—except for the person who must conform.

Some people will love you only if you fit into their box. Don't be afraid to disappoint them. Life isn't about finding yourself; it's about discovering who God created you to be.

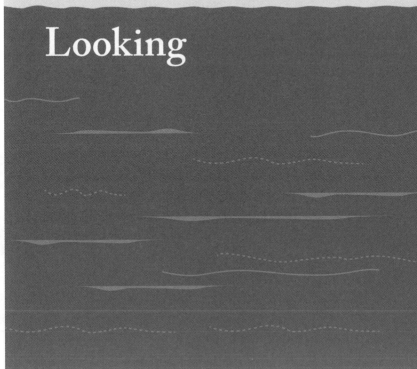

Looking

Upward

CHAPTER 28

Mr. President,
What Did You Say?

When I was seventeen years old, I was honored to be selected as part of a group called the Youth Report to the President. It was 1973, and twelve young people were chosen from across the United States to be in our group.

Of course, I remember visiting the White House quite vividly, especially our time with President Nixon in the Oval Office. The Oval Office is, well, oval. The Presidential Seal is in the middle of the room's carpet, the president's desk backs up to the Rose Garden, and it's quite impressive, as you can imagine.

I stood right next to Nixon during the whole meeting. I remember him being a couple of inches taller than I was and thinking, *This is the most powerful man in the world*. But I'm embarrassed to say I also thought, *He's got the biggest nose I've ever seen, just like the cartoons depict.* But, of course, only a teenager would think that.

Lots of rules applied to us while we were there. For instance, we weren't allowed to ask the president any questions, though he could ask us questions. And plenty of Secret Service people and media were there to cover our meeting, both groups watching our every move, it seemed. Before we met the president, we were taken to places the general public rarely went, such as the floor where the First Family lived and the room where Franklin Roosevelt gave his fireside chats.

Henry Kissinger dropped by, as did John Ehrlichman and H. R. Haldeman, both of later Watergate notoriety. It was a heady experience, but honestly, it was mostly a photo opportunity for the president. Do you remember "the generation gap" of the seventies or have you heard of it? I supposed this meeting made him look like he was bridging that gap.

About nine months earlier, my father had taken me to see Richard Nixon when he was campaigning in the city where I grew up, Fort Wayne, Indiana. Dad noticed the president's press secretary, Ron Ziegler, out in the crowd at this campaign event. He approached Mr. Ziegler to say hello and introduce me. Mr. Ziegler asked us if we would like a gift from the president, and of course we said yes. He promptly gave us each a nice tie clasp with the Presidential Seal and the president's signature on it.

So while in the Oval Office meeting with President Nixon, I was wearing the tie clasp. At the end of our meeting, Nixon asked us if we would like a gift. Of course we all said yes. When he came to me, he reached out to give me the same tie clasp I was wearing, and I told him I already had one.

He laughed and asked me how I got it, so I told him the Ron Ziegler story. He immediately had his aide get me another gift: a beautiful set of cuff links, also with the Presidential Seal. I still have both the tie clasp and the cuff links.

Interestingly, a large photograph of Richard Nixon and me laughing together appeared on the front page of the *Washington Star* (now the *Washington Times*) the following day. That photo is hanging on my office wall behind me as I write this.

Something else happened during our time with the president. As a result of meeting with him that day, I'm on the Oval Office tapes revealed as a result of the Watergate investigation. Here's how I found out.

About a year after I was in the Oval Office, an article in *Newsweek* magazine appeared describing people recorded while there with Richard Nixon. Our group, the Youth Report to the President, was mentioned as one of those groups. And that's how I ended up on the Watergate tapes. Boy, was I surprised.

When I find myself in an unusual place, I'm on the lookout for what God might be up to. It's a holy suspicion that He's at work in my life and in the lives of those around me.

God is like that. He places us somewhere, then does more than we can ask or think.

God wants us to seek Him with our whole hearts. The Bible encourages us when it tells us God said through His prophet Jeremiah, "You will seek Me and find Me, when you search for Me with all your heart" (Jer. 29:13 NKJV).

It's always the right time to seek God. Don't fear the future; God is already there, working on your behalf. God is for you.

Understanding there's more opens you up to *all* God has for you. So we should be asking, "God, why am I here?" in a positive, expectant way. The answer is you're where you are for a reason even if you don't yet know that reason.

So whether you find yourself in a rectangular Wall Street corner office, a square hut in Mongolia, a triangular teepee in Alaska, the Oval Office in the White House, or anywhere else, know there's always more than meets the eye. What you see is only part of the great big story God is writing.

CHAPTER 29

Find the Key That Unlocks Your Destiny's Door

A friend was happy with a project I'd helped him with, but he couldn't pay me in full for it. He said, "I'm really sorry I can't finish paying you, but I have two guitars I can give you instead." Unfortunately, one guitar wasn't in very nice shape, but the other was an Alvarez guitar in good condition.

Thinking this was better than nothing, I accepted the guitars and brought them home, where they sat in our game room for months. Several times I attempted to play the Alvarez, but doing so hurt my fingers, and I didn't have much interest in playing it anyway.

Years went by. My daughter, Michelle, tried playing the guitar on and off, but her interest was more in singing, something she's gifted to do. Then one day, out of the blue, my son Mike took an interest in playing the guitar. He was a young teenager and was growing up fast. And like all young people, he was searching for things to connect with.

I could tell something special was happening to Mike. This guitar, unexpected and in many ways unwanted, had unlocked something inside him. It didn't take long to realize my son had a gift for music, both writing and playing it. For hours almost every day, I could hear Mike upstairs singing and playing songs he'd written.

As a parent, it's always wonderful to see your children discover something that makes their hearts sing. God was doing something in Mike's life and at the same time preparing a way for a future none of us could dream of. The catalyst of it all was that guitar. Mike became involved in the music program in his high school, a highly respected program led by a man named Larry Downey, and was growing in the Lord with his music.

Meanwhile, I continued traveling to speak in churches and at events. One memorable event occurred in Daytona Beach, and I was the main speaker. The music team the host had brought in was a couple who pastored a church in Austin, Texas, and had also founded and were now leading a music college. At the end of the event, they asked if I would be their graduation speaker. I accepted, and later that spring, I gave the graduation address there.

Over dinner after the graduation ceremony, I shared with the pastor and his wife how my son Mike loved singing and playing the guitar and was considering going to a music college in Australia. They listened closely, then said they would love to have him attend their college in Austin—the one where I'd just given the graduation speech.

Mike and I talked about both places. He visited the Austin school, and as he prayed and thought about it, he knew he was supposed to go there.

The college was challenging, and Mike grew in his musical abilities, but I'm not sure that was the main reason God led him there. At the school, he dated a gifted singer named Brittany, and it wasn't long before they were engaged. They married and now have beautiful twin daughters, our granddaughters Emma and Olivia.

This "God story" doesn't end there. Mike is currently the modern worship leader and Brittany is a part of the worship team at a church in Tulsa led by worship arts director Larry Downey, Mike's music teacher from high school.

All this happened because of one guitar—something the giver and the receiver never expected to share.

I like to look at life backward, not with a spirit of regret but in awe at what God was doing when we had no clue. Now I see that God had Mike and Brittany's future in mind when my friend paid me with a guitar.

God orchestrates unexpected things for everybody, including for you right now. He's doing something for your future you don't yet realize. He's working on your behalf today and in the days ahead. He's for you, not against you. So walk out the path He's laid out for you where you are, with what you have.

I believe God will bring "guitars" into your life as catalysts to help you go where He wants you to go and be what He wants you to be. So keep walking, and be open to unexpected blessings, unexpected changes in plans, and unexpected encounters with people. Some people won't alter your destiny, and that's OK. God will put even complete strangers and surprising opportunities on your path to get you where you need to be.

The One who leads you knows where and why He's leading you, and He will give you the keys to unlock your future. Use them and be yourself. When you allow yourself to be you, you create opportunities. The correct key will open the right door. The "guitar" there for you will make beautiful music in your life and in the lives of others.

As I was writing this nugget, I sincerely felt that I should encourage you to pray this simple prayer: "Lord, what is my 'guitar'? Please show me. If I've tried and failed to use it, show me how to begin again. Help me start anew. Hold my hand and my heart as I take the next small step. Thank You, Lord, for Your plan for me. Let it be a blessing to others. In Jesus's name, I pray, amen."

CHAPTER 30

Strength Training

My wife and I decided to have coffee at the local IHOP restaurant. After being seated in a booth near the front, we were quickly greeted by a friendly, happy, smiling waitress. It didn't take long to notice our cheerful helper had only one tooth—on top and smack-dab in the middle. I thought, *Isn't that interesting! Here's a woman with one tooth working in a job that requires a lot of up-close people contact, yet she's smiling, doing a good job.*

Then my eyes were drawn to a button she was wearing that said, "A smile is a gift you can give every day." What a profound scene this was! So much so that I complimented her on her button and sincerely told her she had a nice smile. I wondered if anyone had told her that lately—or ever.

It's good to hunt for the good points in people and then try to do something to help them.

When our waitress returned to refill our coffee cups, she told us her father had done the calligraphy on the button. She said, "He had all his fingers cut off in an industrial accident and *then* decided to pick up calligraphy!" She also said his writing was better than it was before the accident.

I immediately thought, *I guess only a woman who was raised by a dad with no fingers yet who does calligraphy can choose to smile even though she has only one tooth.*

Thomas Edison was afraid of the dark. But he took what he had and made the most of it. His work with electricity and invention of the first practical light bulb took on his fears directly. We should too.

"Strength doesn't come from what you can do. It comes from overcoming the things you once thought you couldn't," observes writer Rikki Rogers.

Don't let the weakness in you affect the greatness in you.

You might have more than one tooth (I certainly hope so), but I promise you have other "deficiencies" that are a part of the perfectly imperfect way God made you.

In 2 Corinthians 12:9–10, the apostle Paul tells us, "[God] has said to me, 'My grace is sufficient for you, for power is perfected in weakness.' Most gladly, therefore, I will rather boast about my weaknesses, so that the power of Christ may dwell in me. Therefore I delight in weaknesses, in insults, in distresses, in persecutions, in difficulties, in behalf of Christ; for when I am weak, then I am strong" (NASB).

Give God your weakness, and He will give you His strength. The Lord does some of His best work with our weaknesses. Sometimes we're tested, not to expose our weaknesses but to discover our strengths.

Never underestimate your strength. Never overestimate your weakness. And don't let either hold you back. Instead, turn them from liabilities into assets. Successful people take what they have, no matter what it looks like, are thankful for what they have, and then go and make the most of it.

CHAPTER 31

When God Stretches You, You Never Return to Your Original Shape

I had just begun to go out and minister in churches, and this was my third official opportunity—speaking in a storefront church in Tampa, Florida, for a bright young pastor. I was naive, inexperienced, excited, and willing to do anything for God. Life was wide open, and I was running full speed ahead.

I spoke to about one hundred people that Sunday night, sharing from my heart as well as I could. Then as I finished my message, I felt I should offer the people an opportunity for prayer at the altar near the front of the sanctuary. Whatever their need, I was going to pray with them about it.

I laid my hands on and prayed for the ten people who came forward. The last person, a young man, asked me to pray for his tongue. I immediately told him to stick it out. Then I grabbed his tongue with my right hand and began to pray for it earnestly. I was probably freaking this kid out, but I went ahead.

After the service, I was outside talking with several church members when the young man with the "tongue issue" came over to me. He clearly spoke and said, "Thank you for praying for me and my tongue. I had a stuttering problem, but God has healed my words tonight."

Wow! God is good. I'll never forget what He did for that boy. But I wonder if I would grab a tongue now that I'm more "experienced" and "wiser." I hope I would if that's what it takes.

Now, weird doesn't equal spiritual. That said, God may ask you to do something way outside your comfort zone. In fact, I promise you He will. Jesus once used spit to heal. God may ask you to get your hands dirty (or wet, in my case) to do His will.

"The scariest paths often lead you to the most exciting places," notes author Lori Deschene. So it's OK to be "spiritually uncomfortable." Because when you are, you're about to do something really, really brave. I've also heard it said, "Don't stay in the boat when God is asking you to walk on water."

I've tried to follow this saying my whole life: "Be instant to obey, taking action without delay." The longer I think, ponder, or even pray about something, the less likely I will do it. The longer it takes to act on God's direction, the more unclear it will become.

"Do one thing every day that scares you," essayist Mary Schmich challenged—and many others have advised the same. Step out of your comfort zone. You're not alone. If God has directed you, He won't leave you hanging.

There might be a tongue out there waiting for you!

CHAPTER 32

Look Who's Coming across Your Path

It was a snowy evening in Fort Wayne, Indiana, when my dad approached me and said, "There's something I want you to be a part of." As a typical teenager, I was automatically uninterested.

He went on. "They meet every Tuesday night downtown at the YMCA."

"Who does? What is this meeting?" I asked.

"It's called Junior Optimist, and it's led by a man I know named Bob Leiman. It's modeled after what adults call Toastmasters. Its purpose is to teach young people how to give speeches."

I certainly had no interest in that! So I was even less interested in the meeting he was asking me to attend. No, more accurately, he was *forcing* me to attend.

The following Tuesday night, driving downtown with my dad was the last thing on earth I wanted to be doing. As we stepped inside the old YMCA, I honestly didn't know what to expect.

When we reached the meeting room, I was thrilled to see it was empty! I thought, *This dumb idea isn't going to happen!*

But the very next day, we discovered we'd shown up on the wrong night. The Junior Optimist club met on Thursdays, not Tuesdays. So the day after that, we took off again to meet with the group I didn't care about.

This time when I walked into the room, it was full of other young people with a rotund man up front. I assumed he was the Bob Leiman who'd arranged all this, the one responsible for my misery. My dad introduced me to him and said he'd pick me up in an hour.

I'll never forget standing in that room and wondering what was about to happen. As a high school athlete, I had no interest in anything outside of sports, but little did I know this unwelcome opportunity would change my life more than any sports team. I had just met the most influential coach of my life.

Bob Leiman was a local high school principal and a professional speaker. He was genuinely interested in young people, especially in teaching them how to stand in front of people and talk. That was why he'd formed this Junior Optimist club. From the start, Mr. Leiman and I connected. He took a personal interest in me.

Soon the weekly meeting I was initially uninterested in was an important part of my life. As I began to learn how to speak in front of people, I realized it came naturally to me. Moreover, since I had a professional speaker as a mentor, I learned things an average fourteen- or fifteen-year-old kid would never know.

Mr. Leiman and the Junior Optimist organization opened doors for me to participate in speech contests. The first one I entered, I won the city contest. Then I won the area contest and ultimately finished second in the state of Indiana. Now I was hooked.

This success eventually led to other opportunities (I gave over eighty speeches while in high school) and one in particular. It was a national speech contest sponsored by *Reader's Digest* and the Boy Scouts of America. I won the city, area, state, and regional competitions and found myself one of twelve regional winners. Our reward included a trip to New York City. I competed there and finished in the top three. No one told us who finished first, second, and third. We just knew the three of us had the opportunity to travel to Washington, DC, to speak in the national finals.

I finished second in the nation and won a scholarship big enough to pay for my first year of college. Since that national contest, I've had the privilege of speaking in person to hundreds of thousands of people, for audiences from fifty to fifteen thousand, all around the world.

All because my dad forced me to do something I had zero interest in doing.

My father wanted something for me that was greater than I could dream for myself, just like our heavenly Father has things for all of us that are so much more than we can even think or dream of. Ephesians 3:20 says, "To Him who is able to do exceedingly abundantly above all that we ask or think, according to the power that works in us" (NKJV).

My dad and Bob Leiman are in heaven now. I'm so thankful for Dad's awareness of this opportunity and persistence and for Mr. Leiman's guidance and vision to bless others. God indeed blesses people through people.

My connection with Mr. Leiman was what I call a "divine connection." I believe with my whole heart that God has these kinds of supernatural relationships for every believer. They can be for something specific in the short run or can last a lifetime. These people come across our paths to impact our destiny and God-given assignments. The Bible is full of these connections: Elijah and Elisha, Paul and Timothy, Moses and Joshua, David and Jonathan, Ruth and Naomi.

These supernatural connections always have two consistent characteristics. First, love for one another—"A friend loves at all times" (Prov. 17:17). And second, others are blessed because of their connection—"As iron sharpens iron, so people can improve each other" (Prov. 27:17 NCV).

Looking back, it's humbling to see how God lined all this up for me. He was directing my steps through my dad and Bob Leiman.

God will place you where He wants you even if no one thinks you should be there. When you submit to Him, He makes this promise to you: "The LORD directs the steps of the godly. He delights in every detail of their lives. Though they stumble, they will never fall, for the LORD holds them by the hand" (Ps. 37:23–24 NLT).

When God gets ready to bless your life, He often sends a person into it—an encouraging friend, a faithful confidant, and maybe a "divine connection."

CHAPTER 33

Help Is on the Way

At one of the most challenging times in my life, I found myself at an evening church service I'll never forget. The worship was so real I genuinely felt the presence of God as I sang to Him. The message was "right on" for my life at that moment, and what was about to happen would change everything for me.

At the end of the service, the minister invited people to come to the altar at the front of the church, where they could pray. I rose from my seat and made my way there. I needed direction, a breakthrough, and so much more. I was walking out Psalm 61:2: "When my heart is overwhelmed . . . lead me to the rock that is higher than I" (NKJV).

As I hit my knees and lifted my voice to God, I didn't know what to specifically pray—though candidly, there was so much I needed to say. But all that could come out of my mouth was, "Help." One word.

As I began to say "Help" repeatedly, my voice became louder, and the depth of that word grew and grew in me. I could literally feel every need, every confession, every issue I needed God's grace and mercy for summed up in that one expression—HELP!

You don't have to talk long for God to know that something is important to you.

As I prayed that simple, one-word prayer, a peace came to me, and a heavy burden was lifted. Right then. Right there. I could feel it. Something changed that night. From that day forward, I was different. Praise God!

It's OK to say we need help. Asking for help that night was one of the most important decisions I've made. I'm still being impacted today by the help God gave me in that moment.

Maybe the right prayer is just saying, "Help me, God! You know my needs, weaknesses, and thoughts before I can even express them." When you ask for help, it's not because you're weak; it's because you want to be strong. Asking for help isn't giving up; it's a sign you're still determined to make it.

The wisest action you can take in any situation is to drop to your knees and ask God for help. Whatever is worth worrying about is certainly worth praying about. Prayer unlocks God's answers and direction. It's OK to say, "I don't know, Lord, but please teach, help, lead, and direct me." God is ready to help you even before you ask. What if it's true that one of the ways to activate His strength in your life is to say, "I don't know, Lord. Please show me"?

My favorite prayer is still one word: *help.* "Help, help, help!"

In his book *Grace for the Moment*, Max Lucado writes, "Do you believe that God is near? He wants you to. He wants you to know that He is in the midst of your world. Wherever you are as you read these words, He is present."[1]

We need a Savior *and* Lord. Why not ask God to help you right now? He certainly wants to.

CHAPTER 34

Advice More Valuable Than a Billionaire's

I've had the privilege to work personally with three billionaires on their books. Two were self-made; the other primarily inherited his money.

When I met my first billionaire, I wondered if something might be different about him. How does a man go from having almost nothing to being worth more than $4 billion in a matter of years, then find himself on the cover of *Inc.* magazine, only to later lose it all and almost go to prison because of a partner's dishonesty? I knew our first conversation would be memorable.

He had reached out because he'd heard about me, my books, my speaking, and my help to authors. I later discovered he was considering writing a book and speaking to business leaders, and he wanted to talk with someone who had successfully done both.

He emailed me, mentioning a mutual friend and requesting a meeting at a local coffee shop. That was how he liked to meet people, I later learned. He would observe how his guest handled their social affairs and how they treated others around them. I arrived a few minutes early, only to find him already waiting in a booth. He always displayed this trait—arriving earlier than anybody he was meeting with—and he was always the first to end the meeting. I took note of both these traits.

After a brief introductory conversation, he looked me in the eye and said, "I know you're religious; I'm not. My book isn't either, but I still value your insight." So began a nearly ten-year relationship.

Bill the billionaire and I would meet many times—at his office, in restaurants, and of course, at the coffee shop. We would talk about business, books, and opportunities. Every time, he would think and strategize higher, wider, and financially bigger than I would, even though I like to think of myself as an "anything is possible" kind of guy. I knew we both put our pants on one leg at a time, but Bill was different. He saw life on a whole other level, in a whole other way. He stretched me.

Sit with winners; the conversation is different.

Let me tell a "Bill story" that demonstrates that. When he began to launch his speaking efforts, he created an audio teaching and workbook revealing some of the secrets to his success. Of course, he priced it about ten times higher than I would have. His first opportunity to stand before an audience and speak was an excellent event hosted by a well-known seminar speaker. The attendees paid a sizable fee to attend, and though already successful, they were hungry, eager to learn, and known to buy teaching products. He spoke on two consecutive weekends.

Bill and I had talked about promoting his product from the stage, and he was eager to speak with me about how it went when he returned. So over breakfast, I asked him about it. He said, "I think it went decent, but I'm not really sure. On the first weekend, I sold $110,000 worth of product, and on the second weekend, $115,000. But, John, I don't have a clue if that's good or bad. What do you think?" He was dead serious.

My jaw dropped. I asked him to repeat that. He impassively did. Right away, I knew his perspective was significantly different from mine even though I was the "expert." I told him those results were incredible, and then I quickly asked how he did it. You can always learn from others, and I wasn't about to miss that opportunity.

When people have been where you can only imagine going, do what you can to learn from them. They see things few others see. They know lessons you can't learn any other way.

Now let me tell you my favorite and most life-changing "Bill story."

Bill continued to speak at events, and we continued to get together. But one day I received an unusual voice mail and email from him. Both said, "I must meet with you as soon as possible!" Bill never presented anything as urgent, so his messages concerned me. Nevertheless, I was hoping everything was OK. Finally, I got ahold of him, and we agreed to meet the following day for breakfast.

I arrived early. Of course, Bill was already there. But something was different. As I walked toward him, he *looked* different. He almost glowed. And the smile on his face was unforgettable.

"I couldn't wait to tell you what happened last weekend, John," he said. "I did my normal speaking, and it went well. But this time, the two hosts asked me if I could stay over and share briefly in a bonus session held Sunday morning. I said yes, thinking I never turn down an opportunity to speak.

"So I showed up for the bonus time Sunday, and the two hosts asked me to read several Scripture passages to the audience. Ben, one of the men, handed me his Bible, and I began to read what they asked me to read. That was it. That was my speaking opportunity."

Bill went on to say that after he finished reading the Bible verses, he sat down as part of the audience listening to the two hosts, Ben Kinchlow (a former host at CBN) and Charlie "Tremendous" Jones (an incredible speaker and author), share about their *real* secret of success—success found in knowing God and His Son, Jesus.

Here's how Bill told me what happened next.

"I had been approached many times about religion, and I always had excellent reasons why I didn't believe or want any part of it. But as I sat there listening, Ben and Charlie started tearing down all my resistance. It was like I'd built a wall, and they were taking the wall down brick by brick. I felt like they were talking only to me, like I was the only person in the room.

"They asked us to close our eyes and repeat a prayer with them, out loud, as they finished. By now, I was all in. I repeated the prayer with everything within me, even though I was concerned that I was speaking the prayer too loudly and I was the only one doing it. I worried I might be in trouble later. But, John, when I prayed that prayer, something happened inside me. I felt different. I had to tell you what happened as soon as I could."

Bill's eyes had watered as he told me about his prayer. Then he sincerely asked, "What did this prayer mean? I've never done or heard of this before."

I told him, "Bill, you prayed a 'sinner's prayer.' God heard you and saw your heart. The Bible says, 'If you confess with your mouth the Lord Jesus and believe in your heart that God raised Him from the dead, you will be saved.' You are now born again. If you died today, you would go to heaven."

This uncommon billionaire had given his life to God. Bill is in heaven today because of two men's actions and a heartfelt prayer.

God can move when you associate with the right people at the right time. The proper place can make the difference between success and failure: impacting others or not making a difference, or spending an eternity separated from God or being with Him forever.

If you find yourself in a position to help someone, like Ben and Charlie did, be grateful and do it. God may be using you to answer someone else's prayers.

Go to God first. He knows what we need when we need it. Trust Him to put you at the right place, at the right time. He might do it at the last minute, but He's never late. Be patient. Everything is working together for your good. Whatever help God has for you is on its way. When He says it's your time, nothing can stop it.

You don't have to have "billionaire advice" to fulfill God's plan for your life. So much more valuable is one word from the Lord through His Word or the Holy Spirit. Or sometimes another person can change everything. Be sure to listen.

If you're still breathing, God is speaking. Obey. Finish your race.

CHAPTER 35

Outlook Determines Outcome

Only a year and a half out of college, I was working in human resources when I decided to enroll in the Master of Business Administration program at the university where I graduated with my undergraduate degree. I had finished three days of classes when I received a surprising phone call from someone I didn't know. He was a recruiter or, as some people say, a "headhunter." He told me about a brand-new job opening and how several people had recommended me as an excellent candidate for it.

I was interested in knowing more, so I asked him to describe everything he could about the job. He told me the position was an assistant to the chairman of the board of the largest bank in Oklahoma, and the bank's human resources department wanted me to interview for it. Although I had just enrolled in the MBA program, this looked like a once-in-a-lifetime op-portunity I shouldn't necessarily pass up.

He described the job as executing special projects for both the chairman and the president, including preparing senior vice presidents and those positioned above for their presentations at the board of directors' meetings. I would interact with state and national business leaders who served on the board and report to the chairman the amount of business each board member brought to the bank each year and any notable activity in their accounts.

The job also included giving speeches on behalf of the pres-ident and the chairman, serving on various local boards on behalf of the bank, overseeing the executive dining program (the bank had its own in-house restaurant for executives and officers of the bank to entertain customers), and overseeing an annual national Association of Tennis Professionals (ATP) tennis tournament the bank jointly owned with a local tennis club. Most of the top tennis players in the world played, and I was responsible for signing their checks, including Jimmy Con-nors's when he won. Last, I would do anything else the chair-man or president wanted. It was an "only-one-in-the-world" job description.

Of course I wanted this job; it was an incredible opportunity, especially for someone as young as me. It wasn't easy to get it, though. I spent the next month interviewing seven times with seven different people, the last two being the bank president and the chairman of the board. I don't know how many other candidates were interviewed, but I was offered the job more than a month later at the end of the process.

I said yes! I had continued attending all my MBA classes during the interview process, but the day I accepted the job, I stepped away from the MBA program to begin my new career in banking.

I had accepted the most nonbanking banking job you could possibly have. And that was just fine with me; I didn't care for accounting or finance subjects in college. But although I didn't know it at the time, the most valuable part of that job would be my opportunity to see, at the age of twenty-four, the view an executive has over the whole organization. I witnessed firsthand their unique pressures, responsibilities, and benefits. This view offered me a perspective most people never get a chance to have. As a result, my view of business, leadership, and opportunity changed forever. Everything looks different when you look at it from the top down instead of from the bottom up.

The bank I was working for was the primary tenant in a fifty-two-story building, and it was designed by the same architect who designed the World Trade Center in New York City—Minoru Yamasaki. Our building looked like an exact replica of those towers, except it was forty-eight stories shorter. On the fifty-second floor was the executive dining area—a beautiful, Italian marble–floored, glass-partitioned place to eat with customers. Because I oversaw this service, I spent many hours looking down and all around from over five hundred feet.

The view frightened some people, while others enjoyed the splendor of seeing the entire city and many of the surrounding suburbs below. It helped me realize I control my perspective and choose what view is in front of me.

Sometimes we need to see from a different perspective to unlock God's plan. Get perspective because the situation might look better from another angle. Change yourself by changing your perspective. Look for the beautiful in unexpected places no one else sees.

You'll never be what you can be if you limit your life to believing the only view that matters is your own. A shift in perspective can create a new reality. When you see things only from your perspective and refuse to be open to other points of view, you could miss what God is trying to teach you or direct you toward. Journalist Al Neuharth observed, "The difference between a mountain and a molehill is your viewpoint."

Here's the perspective God tells us to have: Second Corinthians 4:17 says, "Our present troubles are small and won't last very long. Yet they produce for us a glory that vastly outweighs them and will last forever!" (NLT). So we don't look at the troubles we can see now; rather, we fix our gaze on things that cannot be seen. The things we see now will soon be gone, but the things we can't see will last forever.

What messes up our lives the most is the picture in our heads of how things are "supposed" to be. Our perspective impacts everything—our viewpoint, our way of thinking, our attitude, our outlook, our principles, and our beliefs. "Wisdom is seeing life from God's point of view," says Adrian Rogers in his book *What Every Christian Ought to Know*.[1]

Change your life by changing your viewpoint. You can't watch the sun rise by looking westward. Position yourself to receive all God has for you by seeing your life from His perspective.

CHAPTER 36

Fear Lies

Mom's and Dad's faces beamed as they entered my room. "John, you've been selected to be king of the Kiddie Jamboree." The annual summer jamboree invited all the children in our neighborhood to decorate their bikes, wear costumes, and parade through the streets of our community. Families came out to watch and cheer their friends, relatives, and neighbors.

Each jamboree featured a king and queen wearing crowns and elaborate sashes labeled King or Queen while perched on the back of a convertible and waving to the crowd as they rode the meandering path through every street in the neighborhood.

Picture the annual New Year's Rose Parade done locally. Well, not quite.

Although my parents were happy about my selection, I was not. It was every eight-year-old's worst nightmare. Being the king meant I had to sit beside the *queen*—or more devastatingly, a *girl*! That was the last place I wanted to be. Because girls, as every boy in the 1960s knew, had cooties! Surely the queen would infect me if I had to sit close to her for more than an hour.

Of course, I had to do it because my parents said so. Back then, absolutely no discussion was allowed. So I fulfilled my neighborly duty as the Northcrest King of the Kiddie Jamboree. I wore my crown, my King sash, and a suit, and I waved to the crowd. I didn't actually contract cooties that day, but I feared I would. As far as I can remember, reigning as king of the Kiddie Jamboree was my first encounter with fear. I was experiencing the famous saying "Fear is *False Evidence Appearing Real*."

Today I'm surrounded by all kinds of "cootie carriers"—my wife, daughter, two daughters-in-law, and three cutie-pie grand-daughters. I survive pretty well on that front, but fear still tries to raise its ugly head.

The Bible is our way out of fear. It's our divine advantage anytime we feel bound up by fear and anxiety. Hebrews 4:12 reminds us, "The word of God is living and powerful, and sharper than any two-edged sword, piercing even to the division of soul and spirit, and of joints and marrow, and is a discerner of the thoughts and intents of the heart" (NKJV).

Fear wants to fake us out, steal from us, and disrupt our faith. Fear shouts, *I'm real!* But in nearly every situation, it's not. There is no greater illusion than fear.

Because the Bible is a book about faith, it has a lot to say about fear. Faith and fear have a lot in common. They both believe that what you cannot see will come to pass.

Never trust your fears—they don't know the strength you have with God. Philippians 4:6–7 says, "Don't worry about any-thing; instead, pray about everything. Tell God what you need, and thank him for all he has done. Then you will experience

God's peace, which exceeds anything we can understand. His peace will guard your hearts and minds as you live in Christ Jesus" (NLT).

Being fearful of things going wrong isn't the way to make things go right. What would your life be if you dared to ignore fear and attempt anything? Fear is only temporary; regret lasts forever.

Think about what you might be missing out on if you let fear win by staying in your comfort zone, playing it safe, and not taking the step of faith that could change everything. "God doesn't change His plans to accommodate our fears," notes Pastor Kevin Gerald. Don't let your fears stop you from being great.

I've heard that 365 verses in the Bible deal with fear. One Scripture for each day of the year—a daily answer to the fear you're facing.

Worry is a conversation you have with yourself about things you can't change. Prayer is a conversation you have with God about something He can change.

When fear comes, expect the opposite found in this promise: "God has not given us a spirit of fear, but of power and of love and of a sound mind" (2 Tim. 1:7 NKJV).

Eleanor Roosevelt said, "You gain strength, courage, and confidence by every experience in which you really stop to look fear in the face. You must do the thing which you think you cannot do." Leave your comfort zone. Trust God, and take that step of faith. What He put in your heart to do is waiting for you on the other side of your fears.

CHAPTER 37

Go to Grow

Several years ago, I received a surprise phone call from a man I'd known since college. At the time, he held a prominent position in a well-known but controlling megachurch. He wanted to have lunch with me, and I vividly remember sitting inside a Vietnamese restaurant as he looked straight into my eyes and asked, "How were you able to leave _____ Church?"

Candidly, I was surprised to hear him ask this. I'd always assumed he was the perfect fit for that church. Yet, although he held a significant public presence there, something was missing. He was bored, unexcited. He also faced a major psychological hurdle with the leadership's management style.

This church had an unwritten policy: it didn't bless those who left it. But on the other hand, they would accept anyone who wanted to switch churches and come to theirs. I believe that's called "laws for thee but not for me." Additionally, if someone decided to leave their church, their only response was,

"The door is open when you want to return." And when someone did return to the flock, they would share "testimonies" of people who had left their church only to encounter all kinds of trouble. But these people had returned "home," and now things were much better. The obvious implication was this: Leave, and trouble will come. Stay, and you will be safe.

I remember my friend's worried expression. "That church is not an easy place to leave," I said. "Afterward, some people won't associate with you, and a recording in your head will replay all the upsetting stories you've heard about those who left." But then I assured him. "Yet leaving will absolutely improve your life. You'll discover there's a great big world out there waiting to be significantly influenced by your gifts."

Though I don't know its origin, here's a story often told to make a point.

A father told his daughter, "Congrats on your graduation. I bought you a car awhile back, and I want you to have it now. But before I give it to you, take it to a car dealer in the city and see how much they offer for it."

The girl returned to her father and said, "They offered me only $10,000 because it looks very old."

The father said, "OK, now take it to a pawnshop."

The girl returned to her father and said, "The pawnshop offered only $1,000 for it because it's not only a very old car but also needs a lot of work."

Then the father told her to join a club with experts passionate about cars and show them the car. After a few hours, she returned and told him, "Some people in the club offered me $100,000 because it's a rare car in good condition."

Now the father said, "I want you to know you're not considered worth much if you're not in the right place. If you're not appreciated, don't be angry. That just means you're in the wrong place. Don't stay where no one sees your true value."

Maybe the place where you've been for a long time is no longer the place you belong. Love the people there, forgive them, pray for them, and bless them, but then move on without them. Ecclesiastes 3:1 says, "For everything there is a season, a time for every activity under heaven" (NLT). It's possible to be finished and not be angry or revengeful. Walking away is walking forward. Saying goodbye can unlock the doors God wants us to walk through.

Go. Go where you breathe freely, are respected, and can be yourself. Lose the bad relationship and win your self-respect. I've heard it said, "We don't walk away to teach people a lesson. We walk away because we finally learned ours." Be strong enough to leave and patient enough to allow God to complete the change in you. Run from those who know all your faults but want you to overlook theirs.

Colossians 3:15 has helped me make better decisions. It says, "Let the peace of God rule in your hearts" (NKJV). The word *rule* means "umpire." God's peace can say "out" to inappropriate relationships or "safe" to an opportunity. Pay attention to whether you have God's peace inside you, no matter how good something looks. If you don't have His peace, walk away. It's always better to miss an opportunity than to be involved in something you're not supposed to be involved in.

Dr. Steve Maraboli said, "You can't let people scare you. You can't go your whole life trying to please everyone else. You can't go through life worried about what everyone else is going to think. Whether it's your hair, clothes, what you have to say, how you feel, what you believe and what you have. You can't let the judgment of others stop you from being you. Because if you do, you're no longer you. You're someone everyone else wants you to be."

When there's no longer a reason to stay, it's time to go.

Author Mandy Hale has said, "Growth is painful. Change is painful. But nothing is as painful as staying stuck somewhere you don't belong." Give yourself permission to walk away. Enjoy the sound of your feet walking away from situations no longer meant for you. You must stop watering dead plants.

CHAPTER 38

Lord, Have Mercy

In the late 1980s, I had the privilege of helping a wonderful, growing church in Montgomery, Alabama. The pastor and I really hit it off, and we enjoyed working together as I consulted on strategic planning, job descriptions, marketing, and compensation. He was an out-of-the-box kind of thinker and had hired a great staff. Together, they were doing a great work in the city.

After working all day, he suggested I try a new restaurant that had just come to the area. It wasn't that far from my hotel, and he said the hotel would provide free transportation for me to get there. That sounded great. So upon returning to the hotel, I inquired about that service for breakfast the next morning. The hotel manager walked me outside and pointed to a beautiful stretch limousine. Glistening white, the exceptionally long limo looked brand-new. It was impressive.

Yes, this is what they provided for their guests if they wanted to be taken somewhere. All I had to do was reserve it. I told him I'd like to be taken to a restaurant for breakfast the next day, Saturday morning.

Morning came, and I was excited to go to this place to eat a hearty breakfast before working that day at the church. Down in the lobby, waiting for me was a staff member of the hotel ready to take me in this fantastic limousine.

The driver opened my door, and I settled into the plush leather seat in the back. Now ready to leave, he pushed the button to open the window between us and asked me where I wanted to go. I told him, and off we went.

The restaurant was probably less than five miles away from the hotel, and as we approached it, because we were traveling on a long, winding road, I could see it off in the distance.

I could tell the Cracker Barrel—yes, the Cracker Barrel, a homey chain restaurant many of you know—was quite crowded because people were sitting in the more than twenty rocking chairs out front, and quite a few other people stood. They were all waiting to be called inside. Then I noticed some in the crowd had stopped talking and were gazing in our direction. I thought, *I wonder if they think I'm somebody famous.* It made me laugh.

Sure enough, as we drove up to the front of the restaurant, everybody's eyes turned toward me as the driver got out and opened my door. Then I proudly walked into the restaurant, only to discover I had to wait to get a table, just like "the commoners." All the while, everyone was looking at me, thinking, *Who is this guy?*

Once I was seated, the whole time I was eating my delicious breakfast I noticed several pockets of people looking at me and talking to one another, no doubt trying to figure out who I was. I must admit I was really enjoying this; I love practical jokes.

I had prearranged for the driver to pick me up at a specific time, and when I finished my meal, I had about fifteen minutes left. So I went outside the restaurant, found an empty rocking chair, and sat with the people waiting to get inside for their meal.

I struck up a conversation with the man in the rocking chair next to me. He told me there was a buzz in the restaurant. Rumor had it a famous country western star who'd performed a concert the night before was going to show up there to eat a meal. He'd made it known far and wide that Cracker Barrel was his favorite restaurant.

Soon, out in the far distance, I could see this long, white limousine heading toward the restaurant—and so could everyone else outside. People began to talk, becoming convinced that this famous country western star was heading in their direction, and they couldn't wait to see him. Get his autograph or take a picture. Even the man next to me said he was sure this limo was bringing the celebrity there to eat.

I was getting a kick out of the whole situation. I knew the limo was coming to pick up John, the consultant from Oklahoma, not some famous singer.

I'll never forget the look on everyone's face as the limo pulled up. The driver got out of the vehicle, walked over to me in my rocking chair, and said, "Mr. Mason, are you ready to go?" Every eye was on me as I walked to the back of the limo. I laughed the whole way back to the hotel.

After "being a legend in my own mind" in Montgomery, Alabama, I know things are not always as they appear. In fact, they can sometimes be the opposite of what we see. I'm sure

God mercifully looks at us the same way sometimes—and perhaps chuckles too—thinking, *My child, what's happening is not what you think is happening. I wish you wouldn't worry so much, be so confused, or think this will turn out a certain way instead of trusting that I'm going to take care of My children. Don't let what you think you see make you forget what I've said!*

We all need mercy every day. Thankfully, Lamentations 3:22–23 says, "Through the LORD's mercies we are not consumed, because His compassions fail not. They are new every morning; great is Your faithfulness" (NKJV). This morning you and I received new mercy from God. Don't we all need a little more mercy and grace?

Nothing is as it appears. A different version of you exists in the mind of everyone who knows you—just like you see people differently from how they see themselves. Let that lead you to extend more mercy and grace to others.

Here's another story, told in slightly different versions.

A little silver-haired lady calls her neighbor and says to him, "Please come over here and help me. I have a killer jigsaw puzzle, and I can't figure out how to get started."

Her neighbor asks, "What is it supposed to be when it's finished?"

The little silver-haired lady says, "According to the picture on the box, it's a rooster."

Her neighbor decides to go over and help with the puzzle. She lets him in and shows him where she has the puzzle spread all over her table. He studies the pieces for a moment, then looks at the box before turning to her and saying, "First of all, no matter what we do, we won't be able to assemble these pieces into anything resembling a rooster."

Then he takes her hand and kindly says, "Second, I want you to relax. Let's have a nice cup of tea, and then," he says with a deep sigh, "let's put all the cornflakes back in the box."

Like this neighbor had mercy on the older lady, let's you and I express how God lives in us by extending uncommon mercy to others. Tomorrow, you could be standing next to someone trying the best they can to keep their life from falling apart. Jude 1:22 says, "You must show mercy to those whose faith is wavering" (NLT). When we look at ourselves and others, we realize we all need mercy—and as much unmerited grace as we can receive.

Matthew 5:7 says, "Blessed are the merciful, for they will receive mercy" (NASB). Why don't you share some of the mercy you've been given with someone today? As you do, mercy will come back to you. Remember, "The Lord is good; His mercy is everlasting" (Ps. 100:5 NKJV). So let's receive and share His new, everlasting mercy today. We all certainly need it.

CHAPTER 39

Saved by a Question

It was a beautiful Sunday morning in Fort Wayne, Indiana, and my family had risen early to attend the service at Memorial Baptist Church. We'd been members there for several years.

We sat together on the right side of the sanctuary, about halfway back—almost in the front row for a Baptist church. I remember wearing my very favorite shoes, my penny loafers. This style of shoes was popular, and as a twelve-year-old, I was proud to own a pair. I was determined to wear them everywhere I could even though my constant use had caused some stitching along the top of my right shoe to come undone. As a result, my white sock was poking out. But despite the wardrobe malfunction, nothing was going to stop me from wearing those shoes.

Nothing about the service was remarkable that morning, but something was about to happen that would change my life forever. First, I listened to the sermon. Then as Pastor Richard Mitchell concluded his message, he looked out at the congregation and posed this question: "If you were to die tonight, do you know for certain you would go to heaven?"

I'm sure I'd heard this question many times before, but it hit me differently on this day in the summer of 1967. As I heard Pastor Mitchell's words, my heart opened. The pastor continued by saying, "If you accept Jesus Christ as your personal Lord and Savior, you will know today, right now, that you will go to heaven. If you would like to receive Jesus, I invite you to come to the front of the sanctuary and publicly declare it."

Without hesitation, I stood, stepped into the center aisle, and walked forward toward Pastor Mitchell. As I did, I noticed my white sock, visible to all. But nothing was going to stop me.

Looking back, I know the Holy Spirit was drawing me to God, and what was happening was deeply real to me. I made my decision to accept Christ that morning because of the powerful question my pastor asked everyone in the service.

I'm thrilled I answered my pastor's question the way I did because Jesus has made all the difference in my life.

Our answers to questions make a difference not only for all eternity but also for good and bad here on earth. You're where you are today because of the questions you've asked yourself and others. To get where you want to be, you must ask the right questions. The difference between uncommon people and common people is that uncommon people ask better questions and therefore get better results.

That's how we can discover life's most important answers—from questions. Asking questions is a sure way to learn, grow, and find the answers we're looking for. Asking questions was used by the greatest teacher of all, Jesus. In the New Testament, it's recorded that He asked more than 150 questions. I like to say, "He's the answer, but He's also asking all the questions."

Be uncommon by asking these twenty-one Jesus questions:

1. "Look at the birds. They don't plant or harvest or store food in barns, for your heavenly Father feeds them. And aren't you far more valuable to him than they are?" (Matt. 6:26 NLT).
2. "If you love those who love you, what reward will you get?" (Matt. 5:46).
3. "Why do you look at the speck of sawdust in your brother's eye and pay no attention to the plank in your own eye?" (Matt. 7:3).
4. "Why do you break the command of God for the sake of your tradition?" (Matt. 15:3).
5. "Who do you say I am?" (Matt. 16:15).
6. "What do you benefit if you gain the whole world but lose your own soul? Is anything worth more than your soul?" (Matt. 16:26 NLT).
7. "Have you never read in the Scriptures?" (Matt. 21:42).
8. "How will you escape being condemned to hell?" (Matt. 23:33).
9. "Why are you so afraid? Do you still have no faith?" (Mark 4:40).
10. "Why are you thinking these things in your hearts?" (Luke 5:22).
11. "Why do you call me, 'Lord, Lord,' and do not do what I say?" (Luke 6:46).
12. "Where is your faith?" (Luke 8:25).

13. "However, when the Son of Man comes, will he find faith on the earth?" (Luke 18:8).

14. "What do you think? If a man has a hundred sheep, and one of them has gone astray and gets lost, will he not leave the ninety-nine on the mountain and go in search of the one that is lost?" (Matt. 18:12 AMPC).

15. "Who of you by worrying can add a single hour to your life?" (Luke 12:25).

16. "Jesus knew what they were thinking, so he asked them, 'Why do you have such evil thoughts in your hearts?'" (Matt. 9:4 NLT).

17. "Do you believe that I am able to do this?" (Matt. 9:28).

18. "And He said to them, 'Why are you disturbed and troubled, and why do such doubts and questionings arise in your hearts?'" (Luke 24:38 AMPC).

19. "What do you think of the Christ? Whose Son is He?" (Matt. 22:42 AMPC).

20. "What do you want me to do for you?" (Matt. 20:32). Seven other times in the New Testament, Jesus asked, "What do you want?"

21. "Do you love me?" (John 21:17).

What questions are shaping your life? No matter what area of your life you want to improve, you can ask questions that will provide you with the right answers. Life's most important answers can be found in asking the right questions.

CHAPTER 40

What If It's True?

John!" I heard a familiar voice shouting. It was Bill.

I was standing in the parking lot of the school where I once was the head basketball coach. I knew Bill as the stepfather of a young man who had played basketball for me. His son was the kind of kid who would dive on the floor for the ball, take charges, and give 100 percent every minute he was in the game—the type of player every coach wanted.

Bill was a great man too. He had a background in business and had experienced a rather radical conversion to Christ. Because of his leadership skills, a prominent local Bible institute named him the director of the entire school.

As Bill walked toward me, he said, "I need to talk to you about something."

Well, I was all ears.

"John, I would like you to teach a course on faith."

You need to understand that I live in a city known for faith teaching. In fact, we have a large Bible college primarily built around teaching faith. The Bible institute where he asked me to teach this course was also known for its strength in teaching faith.

I must admit that I laughed, wondering if this was some kind of prank. My first response was, "You're kidding, right?"

"No. I'm very serious. I think you'd be perfect for teaching this class. I believe you're the right one God has for this."

I paused for a moment, feeling completely unqualified. And ironically, I knew it would require faith for me to even assume I could do it. So I told him I needed to think and pray about it.

I walked away feeling that, somehow, this was something I should do. I knew God had never had anybody qualified working for Him yet, and I certainly fit that bill. *But*, I wondered, *what if what Bill said is true? What if God has chosen me for this?*

It didn't take me long to get back to Bill with my decision. I said yes. I knew I was supposed to do it even though I had no experience or credentials. I did, however, have direction as to how I should teach this course. So I told Bill, "I will teach the class on faith under one condition: that I can also teach about love and works." I knew the Bible teaches that faith works through love (Gal. 5:6) and that faith without works is dead (James 2:17). I wasn't about to teach a course on faith without including the whole truth.

I taught the course, or maybe I should say the course taught me. The students responded well, and something good happened inside me.

A minister friend of mine used to say, "What if it's true?" when referring to the Scriptures. When you consider that question, at first it sounds like doubt. Instead, isn't that a statement a person walking by faith could ask?

I believe that kind of spiritual hopefulness is an excellent way to live your life. What would happen if you applied that question in a positive way, not in a doubtful way? I believe your faith would grow and that opportunities you would never have seen without that question would come your way.

Think about it. What if it's true that

- God wants you to prosper and be in health, even as your soul prospers (3 John 1:2).
- Nothing can separate you from God's love for you (Rom. 8:39).
- God works everything together for good (Rom. 8:28).
- God gives you wisdom (James 1:5).
- God will protect you (Ps. 91:2).
- God will meet all your needs (Phil. 4:19).
- God is faithful (Josh. 1:9).
- God is ready to forgive your sins (Ps. 86:5).
- You can trust God (Heb. 10:23).
- God is your strength (Phil. 4:13).
- God's compassion is new every morning (Lam. 3:23).
- God created you for a purpose (Eph. 2:10).
- Jesus wants you to have an abundant life (John 10:10).
- Jesus hears your prayers (John 14:13–14).
- God gives you peace (John 14:27).
- God provides a way out of trouble (1 Cor. 10:13).
- God provides us with a solution to fear (1 Pet. 5:7).

- God loves you (1 John 4:9–10).
- God promises you everlasting life (John 3:16).

If you're going to believe everything you read, start with the Bible. God makes more than seven thousand promises to you and me in His Word. Are they true? Here's the answer: "All the promises of God in Him are Yes, and in Him Amen, to the glory of God through us" (2 Cor. 1:20 NKJV).

Think about it. What if it's true God wants you to be uncommon?

Be Uncommon

Don't allow yourself to be at the bottom of the top, the best of the worst, the top of the bottom, and the worst of the best. Use the talents God gave you; don't bury them. The best thing about the future is that it starts tomorrow. So abandon the common life and live the uncommon life God planned for you. Now is the time to be uncommon.

Live authentically.
Grow continuously.
Celebrate people.
Hope for the best.
Watch your words.
Choose to forgive.
Laugh every day.
Worship the King of Kings.
Live by faith.
Serve others.
Talk to God.
Listen to God.
Give your all.

Be free.
Walk humbly.
Trust God always.
Tell others the Good News.
Love God, and love others.

Notes

Introduction

1. Vocabulary.com, s.v. "common," accessed July 11, 2022, https://www.vocabulary.com/dictionary/common.

Chapter 4 Stay Off the Slippery Slope

1. Joyce Meyer, *Making Good Habits, Breaking Bad Habits: 14 New Behaviors That Will Energize Your Life* (Nashville: FaithWords, 2013), 7.

Chapter 10 To Tell the Truth

1. "Telling the truth when tempted to lie can significantly improve a person's mental and physical health, according to a 'Science of Honesty' study presented at the American Psychological Association's 120th Annual Convention." Lead author Anita E. Kelly, PhD, professor of psychology at the University of Notre Dame, reveals, "We found that the participants could purposefully and dramatically reduce their everyday lies and that in turn was associated with significantly improved health." See "Lying Less Linked to Better Health, New Research Finds," American Psychological Association, accessed August 1, 2022, https://www.apa.org/news/press/releases/2012/08/lying-less.

Chapter 11 Where You Are Is the Best Place to Start

1. Stephen King, *On Writing: A Memoir of the Craft* (New York: Scribner, 2000), 269.

Chapter 12 Different Is the Difference

1. Kurt Vonnegut, *Player Piano* (New York: The Dial Press, 1999), 84.

Chapter 13 Keep Swinging

1. Keely Levins, "Want to Know Your Odds for a Hole-in-One? Well, Here They Are," Golf Digest, November 8, 2013, https://www.golfdigest .com/story/want-to-know-your-odds-for-a-hole-in-one-well-here-they-are.

2. Joe Gillard, "Ronald McNair, the Boy Who Refused to Leave the Library," *History Hustle*, March 28, 2020, https://historyhustle.com/ronald -mcnair/.

Chapter 23 Success Is a Series of Small Wins

1. Robin Sharma (@RobinSharma), "The way we do small things determines the way we do everything," Twitter, August 24, 2015, 11:55 a.m., https:// twitter.com/robinsharma/status/635842855106408448?lang=en.

2. *The Hobbit*, directed by Peter Jackson (Burbank, CA: Warner Bros. Pictures, 2012).

Chapter 26 I Forgive You—Goodbye

1. Rick Warren, *God's Power to Change Your Life* (Grand Rapids: Zonder-van, 2008), 53.

Chapter 33 Help Is on the Way

1. Max Lucado, *Grace for the Moment: Morning and Evening Devotional Journal* (Nashville: Thomas Nelson, 2013), 157.

Chapter 35 Outlook Determines Outcome

1. Adrian Rogers, *What Every Christian Ought to Know: Solid Grounding for a Growing Faith* (Nashville: B&H, 2012), 165.

Author Contact

John Mason welcomes the opportunity to speak at churches, conferences, and various business settings. For more information, to schedule John Mason to speak, or for author coaching and publishing services, please contact:

John Mason
Insight International
contact@freshword.com
www.freshword.com
918-493-1718

If you have any prayer needs,
please don't hesitate to contact us.
It's a privilege to pray for you.

John Mason is an internationally recognized bestselling author, speaker, minister, and author coach. He's the founder and president of Insight International and Insight Publishing Group, organizations dedicated to helping people reach their dreams and fulfill their God-given destiny.

He has authored thirty-two books, including *An Enemy Called Average*, *You're Born an Original—Don't Die a Copy!*, *Let Go of Whatever Holds You Back*, and *Know Your Limits—Then Ignore Them*, which have sold over two million copies and have been translated into more than forty languages throughout the world. His books are widely known as sources of godly wisdom, scriptural motivation, and practical principles. His writings have been published in *Reader's Digest* and numerous other national publications. In addition, seven of his books have reached the #1 spot on an Amazon bestseller list.

Known for his quick wit, powerful thoughts, and insightful ideas, he is a popular speaker across the US and around the world.

John and his wife, Linda, have four children: Michelle, Greg, Michael, and David, and five grandchildren: Emma, Olivia, Beckett, Darby, and Briggs.

Find More Wisdom from

John Mason

freshword.com |

Don't Let Your Thoughts
LIMIT YOUR POTENTIAL